IRISH REGIONAL DEVELOPMENT

IRISH REGIONAL DEVELOPMENT

A New Agenda

Edited by Eoin O'Leary

The Liffey Press

Published by
The Liffey Press Ltd
Ashbrook House, 10 Main Street
Raheny, Dublin 5, Ireland
www.theliffeypress.com

A catalogue record of this book is
available from the British Library.

ISBN 1-904148-37-9

Printed in the Republic of Ireland by Colour Books Ltd.

*This book has been sponsored by the Association of Irish Regions,
which is the national representative organisation for the eight
Regional Authorities and the two Regional Assemblies.*

CONTENTS

ACKNOWLEDGEMENTS

This book is dedicated to Robert Garhart, from the University of St Thomas in Minnesota, who sadly passed away in 1999 at too young an age. Some years ago Bob got me interested in regional economics, during his two, year-long sabbaticals at UCC. We worked very closely together during the mid-1990s in constructing a regional model of the South-West. Bob was a respected member of the regional science community and got me interested in attending regional science conferences around the world. He was a great colleague and a very nice person.

The idea for the book grew out of discussions I initially had with Connell Fanning, Professor of Economics at UCC during 2001. I would like to thank Connell for his foresight and his perseverance in convincing me of the increasing and widespread interest in Irish regional issues. I then proceeded to organise a symposium entitled "A New Agenda for Irish Regional Development" held in UCC in September 2002, the success of which led me to editing this book.

Neither the book nor the symposium would have existed without the contributed chapters. I am therefore especially grateful to the authors who agreed, sometimes without even knowing me beforehand, to present a paper at the symposium and subsequently to write chapters for this book. I have greatly enjoyed working with each of them as the book took shape. I would like to thank them for their enthusiasm for the project, for their punctuality in meeting my deadlines over the past 15 months and for the quality of their contributions. It has been a pleasure to work with them. Thanks also to David Givens of The

Liffey Press for his assistance and professionalism in producing the final product.

I am also greatly indebted to the Association of Irish Regions for providing funding for the book. In discussing the idea in January 2002 with John McAleer, the Regional Director of the South-West region, John suggested that the Association might be willing, in addition to funding the symposium, to also provide sponsorship for this book. I am grateful to John for his foresight. This idea received considerable support from Jim Stone, the Honorary Secretary of the Association and Tom Byrne, the Regional Director of the South-East region. I would like to express my sincere thanks to each of these and, indeed, to all of the Directors of the Regional Authorities for their support.

Funding for the symposium was also received from the British and Irish Section of the Regional Science Association International, which is one of the leading international associations for research in regional issues. Thanks to John Dewhurst, Graham Clarke, Mike Danson, Ron McQuaid, Dimitris Ballas and the sections other committee members for their support. Thanks also to the Faculty of Arts in UCC, and in particular to Professor Peter Woodman, Dean of Arts, for providing funding. The success of the symposium was also due to adept chairing by Mr John O'Brien, Special Advisor to the Tánaiste and Minister for Enterprise and Employment, Ms Mary Harney. I am extremely grateful to John for making time from his busy schedule to chair the event.

I would like to express thanks to my colleagues in the Department of Economics, UCC. Thanks to my co-authors, Ed and Ella for their ongoing support. Thanks also to our Department Manager, Mary Maguire and her staff, especially Paula Cashman and Dympna O'Donovan for their help.

Finally, a special thanks to Maeve, Emma and Kate for being there.

Eoin O'Leary
University College Cork
August 2003

FOREWORD

The issue of regional development is very topical in Ireland at present. The recent publication of the National Spatial Strategy: 2002–2020 shows the commitment by the Irish government to regional issues, which are increasingly becoming part of the public debate. The next number of decades are likely to present significant challenges to Irish policymakers at local, regional and national levels, to address the increasing disparities in living standards that are already emerging in Irish regions. Appropriate regional policies are particularly needed in order to provide a better quality of life for Irish people, to sustain economic competitiveness and to improve the quality of our environment.

The Association of Irish Regions is very closely involved in the formulation of Irish regional policy. The Association is the national representative organisation of the eight Regional Authorities and two Regional Assemblies. The main functions of Regional Authorities are to co-ordinate the provision of public services in the regions, to review regional development requirements and to make submissions to government for EU financial assistance. The Regional Assemblies were formed in 1999 following the regionalisation arrangements negotiated by the Irish government. The membership of the assemblies is drawn from the Regional Authorities. The Association offers advice to government on any matters pertaining to the economic and social development of the State or any region thereof, including any matters pertaining to balanced regional development. It facilitates exchange of information between members of regional authorities. It also arranges meetings, conferences, seminars and publications to further its aims.

The Association is strongly of the view that in facing the challenges ahead, regional policymakers require thought provoking analysis from researchers in a number of disciplines. Although economic researchers have been prominent in proffering advice on national economic issues, the economics profession in Ireland has not been as evident in the emerging regional debate. Yet, as a discipline economics has much to offer, by way of rigorous analysis of the choices faced in Irish regions, not just on issues such as human and physical infrastructure that underpin economic competitiveness, but also on related issues such as quality of life.

The Association of Irish Regions is therefore delighted to sponsor this book, which draws together, under one cover, internationally respected, mostly Irish-based economists, who are working in the area of Irish regional development. The book succeeds in setting a new agenda for thinking about the regional policy dilemma, the issue of regional growth and innovation and the infrastructural deficit. We recommend it to regional lobbyists, public servants, policymakers and the general public who are involved and interested in Irish regional issues. We also recommend it to researchers, teachers and students in the areas of economics, business, geography and planning.

The catalyst for the book has been Dr Eoin O'Leary of the Department of Economics at UCC, who has been working on Irish regional development since the mid-1990s. At the request of John McAleer, the Regional Director of the South-West region, Eoin met a number of our directors in early 2002 to discuss an article on the Irish regional policy dilemma which he had recently published in the *Irish Banking Review*. During this meeting, the idea first surfaced for a symposium followed by a book setting a "New Agenda for Irish Regional Development". Eoin has succeeded in drawing together an impressive array of contributors, who have managed to present very accessible and interesting analyses of the key areas in Irish regional development.

The Association is delighted to have been involved in this extremely worthwhile book.

Jim Stone, Honorary Secretary
The Association of Irish Regions
July 2003

LIST OF TABLES AND FIGURES

ABOUT THE CONTRIBUTORS

Eoin O'Leary (Editor and Chapters 1, 2 and 10)

Eoin has been a lecturer in the Department of Economics at UCC since 1992, after previous careers in Waterford IT and the CSO. He obtained his PhD in 1995 for the study of EU convergence. He has published numerous papers on EU and more recently Irish regional convergence in a variety of international journals, such as *Regional Studies* and the *International Regional Science Review*. He is also the author of a recent paper in the *Irish Banking Review*, "Regional Divergence in the Celtic Tiger: The Policy Dilemma", which was covered by a number of national newspapers. Eoin is a committee member of the Regional Science Association International, British and Irish Section. He has undertaken substantial consultancy work for various businesses in the South-West, using the only survey-based regional input-output model of an Irish region. His teaching duties are in the areas of economic growth, innovation and regional economics.

Bernadette Andreosso-O'Callaghan (Chapter 7)

Bernadette is Jean Monnet Professor of Economic Integration and Director of the Euro-Asia Centre, University of Limerick. She is a graduate of the College of Europe (Brugge, Belgium) as well as of the Universities of Paris (Panthéon Sorbonne) and Lille (Sciences et Techniques). She is currently visiting researcher and Professor at the Paul Valéry University of Montpellier, and at Seoul National University. Her major research interests are in the area of economic integration, with a particular focus on EU-Asia relations, and on structural and technologi-

Irish Regional Development

cal change in European and Asian countries. She has published numerous scholarly articles, including research on innovation systems in the Shannon region.

Mike Danson (Chapter 3)

Mike is Professor of Scottish and Regional Economics at the University of Paisley, Scotland. He is Chair of the Regional Studies Association, editor of "Debates & Surveys" in the journal *Regional Studies*, and committee member of the Regional Science Association International: British & Irish Section. He has researched and advised widely for local and central governments (undertaking the first ever research for the Scottish Parliament), trades unions and community groups, on a range of subjects, including regional development agencies, regional economic restructuring, small business development, land reform, local taxation, clusters and the Scotch Whisky industry. He is currently on secondment to Future Skills Scotland, looking at employability issues. He recently became a member of the Academy of Learned Societies for the Social Sciences.

John Dewhurst (Chapter 4)

John is a Chartered Statistician and holds the Chair in Regional Economics at the University of Dundee. He has previously held visiting positions at the University of Queensland and Kansas State University. His research interests lie in the application of economic statistics to regional and inter-regional matters. He is currently working on the relationships between industrial structure, inter-regional trade and regional growth. He is an active member of the Regional Science Association International. He is the immediate past Chairman of the British and Irish Section, he has served as European editor of "Papers in Regional Science" — the association's journal — and is currently an elected member of the World Council of the association.

Nola Hewitt-Dundas (Chapters 6 & 7)

Nola is First Trust Bank Senior Lecturer in Innovation in the School of Management and Economics at Queens University, Belfast. Her main research interests focus on innovation and new technology adoption by small firms and company benchmarking. She has wide experience of policy evaluation and has worked on consultancy assignments for a range of public sector agencies in Northern Ireland and the Republic of Ireland. Nola graduated from Queen's University, Belfast before undertaking doctoral research on company flexibility in Ireland and the USA. She has published two books, numerous research articles and research reports on innovation and related subjects.

Rachel Hillard (Chapter 8)

Rachel is a lecturer in strategic management at NUI, Galway. Her research interests are in the field of innovation, technical change and organisational capabilities. Her recently completed PhD research looks at the role of organisation capabilities in determining industry response to technology-forcing environmental regulation.

David Jacobson (Chapter 8)

David teaches economics and political economy at Dublin City University Business School. His research focuses on industrial and regional economics. He has published, among others, studies of the furniture industry in County Monaghan and the software manual printing industry in Dublin. His industrial policy work includes studies for Enterprise Ireland and, on specifically regional issues; he has recently contributed on Industrial Agglomeration to the *Handbook of Economics*. His textbook (with Bernadette Andreosso-O'Callaghan) on *Industrial Economics and Organization: A European Perspective* emphasises the spatial aspects of industrial development. He is currently involved in a number of EU Fifth Framework Programme studies.

Ella Kavanagh (Chapter 10)

Ella has been a lecturer in the Department of Economics at UCC since 1990. She obtained her MA degree from UCC and her PhD from the University of Strathclyde in 1995. The topic of her PhD was the choice of exchange rate regime for small countries in which she explored the impact of the exchange rate regime on inflation performance. She has published chiefly in the area of open economy macroeconomics with specific reference to small countries. Most recently she has had a paper published with Professor Liam Gallagher in the *Manchester School* on "Real and Nominal Shocks to Exchange Rates: does the Regime matter?" She has participated in consultancy work for various businesses in the South-West. Her teaching areas include macroeconomics, international finance and international macroeconomics.

Michael Keane (Chapter 11)

Michael is Associate Professor of Economics at the National University of Ireland, Galway. His teaching and research interests are spatial economics, regional and local development and tourism. In 1996 he wrote (with P. Commins, Teagasc) *NESC 97, New Approaches to Rural Development*. He has published papers in the *Journal of Regional Science, Regional Studies* and *Environment and Planning A*. He is a member of the Regional Science Association. Current research includes Spatial Labour Markets, an Evaluation of Rural Tax Designation Schemes, Networking Strategies for Local Development and an ERDF-funded project on Social Accounting Systems in collaboration with the Letterkenny Institute of Technology and Professor Tom Johnson, University of Missouri, USA.

Jim Love (Chapter 6)

Jim is Professor of Economics and International Business, Aston Business School, Aston University, Birmingham. He graduated from the University of Strathclyde before undertaking doctoral research on the structure of the Scottish whisky industry. Jim's research interests span industrial economics and international business with a particular emphasis on technology transfer and innovation. He has published widely in both areas and with Brian Ashcroft is the author of the definitive study of takeover and merger activity in the Scottish economy. Jim is head of the Strategic Management and Innovation group within Aston Business School.

Edgar Morgenroth (Chapter 5)

Edgar has been Research Officer at the Economic and Social Research Institute since 1998. He received his Bachelor's degree (Economics and Geography) and Master's degree (Economics and Finance) from the National University of Ireland, Maynooth, and carried out his Doctoral research at Keele University in the UK. He is also an alumni of Boston College, having completed the Urban Economic Development Program in Boston (MA) and Portland, Oregon during 2001. Before joining the ESRI he worked as a teaching assistant at both NUI Maynooth and Keele University. Edgar is chairman of the Committee of the Regional Studies Association, Irish Branch and a board member of the Regional Studies Association. His research interests include the determinants of economic growth both at a national and regional level, the determinants of firm location, regional disparities, regional policy and the returns and efficiency of public investment. Edgar has completed projects such as an ex-ante evaluation of investment needs for Ireland, evaluations of the macroeconomic and regional impact of EU Structural Funds, and a major study on the regional economic profile of the Greater Dublin Region. He is currently part of a consortium of leading international research institutes that have been awarded funding under the EU Fifth Framework to carry out research on the Impact of European Integration and Enlargement on Regional Structural Change and Cohesion.

John Murray (Chapter 7)

John completed a Master of Business Studies in the University of Limerick in 2000. He has worked on projects including an EU-funded cross-comparative study of 12 peripheral regions. John has also participated in an examination of technology and knowledge transfer activity between multinational enterprises and their indigenous suppliers in Northern Ireland and in the Republic of Ireland. Innovation systems, knowledge management, customer relationship management, Asian business/economic developments are included among his research interests. He is currently a Research Project co-ordinator on the Retail Sector in Dublin Institute of Technology, and is also engaged with the DIT TRAMs research team, which investigates the responses of firms to adopting e-business initiatives.

Aisling Reynolds-Feighan (Chapter 9)

Aisling graduated from University College Dublin with BA (1985) and MA (1986) degrees in Economics. She holds a Ph.D. degree from the University of Illinois at Urbana-Champaign in the field of Regional Science. She has been a member of the Economics Department at University College Dublin since 1989, where she teaches courses in transport economics, regional science and microeconomics. Her main research interests are in air and road transport economics and logistics. Aisling has published widely on comparative US and European air transportation systems, networks and policies. She is a committee member of the Air Transport Research Society (of the World Conference on Transport Research) and European Councillor for the Regional Science Association International. She has undertaken consultancy work for the Irish Department of Public Enterprise, European Commission, US DOT, OECD, and several Irish research institutes. Aisling is Director of UCD's Transport Policy Research Institute.

Stephen Roper (Chapters 6 & 7)

Stephen is Professor of Business Innovation at Aston Business School, Aston University, Birmingham. Prior to joining Aston University, Stephen was Assistant Director of the Northern Ireland Economic Research Centre, Belfast. Stephen's research and teaching activities centre on innovation, small business and regional development. He has published widely in each area and has led a series of projects designed to benchmark innovation activity in Irish businesses in an international context. Stephen has undertaken consultancy assignments for government departments and agencies throughout Ireland and the UK, and was recently part of an OECD expert panel compiling a report on the Helsinki ICT cluster.

Edward Shinnick (Chapter 10)

Edward has been a lecturer in the Department of Economics at UCC since 1993. He received his BA degree (Economics and Mathematics) and Master's degree (Economics) from University College Cork. He received his PhD from the University of Strathclyde in 1999. His research interests lie in the area of Business Economics with a focus on competition, regulation and privatisation issues, where he has published a number of papers in international journals. The most recent of which identifies a series of regional markets for legal services and is published in *Regional Studies*. In addition he has carried out consultancy projects for a number of firms in the South-West region.

Chapter 1

INTRODUCTION

Eoin O'Leary

Ireland has undergone dramatic change in the last ten to fifteen years. We have gone from being one of Europe's underachievers to a "tiger economy", the envy of other small countries. During the 1990s phenomenal annual average growth of 7-8 per cent resulted in Ireland catching up on the EU norm. Employment increased by a massive 37 per cent during the decade, with the result that Ireland's historically large unemployment problem seemed no more. Although, from the outside, the headline statistics drew much attention, it was clear from the public debate emerging throughout the 1990s that to many citizens all was not as it seemed. Problems were emerging, some of which had the potential to undermine continued prosperity of the country.

This book is concerned with the emergence of a "regional problem". Regional inequality has been increasing in Ireland, with rural areas being left behind due to the economic might of the country's urban centres, especially Dublin and to a lesser extent Cork and Limerick. At the same time rising house prices and traffic congestion are choking the economic life out of the nation's cities, especially Dublin. The main objective of the book is to highlight, in a readable and accessible manner, the contribution that the economics profession can make to understanding and addressing these problems. To date, an economic perspective has been somewhat lacking in the Irish regional debate. In gathering together eminent economists who have something to add to our thinking about these problems, the book aims to set a new agenda for Irish regional development.

The book is targeted at two broad types of readers. The first are lobbyists, public servants, policymakers and the general public who are involved and interested in Irish regional issues. In the recent past a number of regional lobbies, like the Western Development Commission, have been formed and have attracted much public support, as evidenced by the election of Ms Marian Harkin to the Sligo/Leitrim constituency in the recent general election. Such groups increasingly interact with public servants and policymakers involved in various bodies and fora such as Enterprise Boards, County and City Councils, the IDA and Government Departments. It is hoped that this book will be of use to each of these groups and the general public as they enter into dialogue about regional issues.

The second target market includes researchers, teachers and students in the areas of economics, business, geography and planning. Although written by economists, the books non-technical and accessible style makes it attractive to those specialising in other disciplines besides economics. There are increasing numbers of regional specialists working in government departments and agencies, research institutes, consultancies and third level institutions, both in Ireland and in other countries, who are working in the increasingly topical area of Irish regional development. In addition, students in Irish universities, Institutes of Technology and other colleges who are, in increasing numbers, opting for final year undergraduate or postgraduate courses in such areas as economic growth and development, regional/business competitiveness, human geography and urban and rural planning, might also use the book.

This introduction continues by first outlining the emerging regional debate as reflected in political and media commentaries. It then identifies the kinds of insights that economists can provide on these issues. It concludes by outlining the structure of the book and the contributions of the chapters.

THE EMERGING REGIONAL DEBATE

During the 1990s, it became increasingly clear that the prosperity generated by the "Celtic Tiger" was not being distributed evenly throughout the regions. The most prosperous regions, like Dublin and to a lesser extent other urban centres, were seen to be benefiting more than the poorer predominantly rural regions. Thus, between 1993 and 1999, while household income per capita in Dublin/Mid-East increased by 5.6 per cent annually, the Midlands registered growth of only 2.9 per cent per annum (O'Leary, 2002/3).[1]

In the policy arena, this widening of the gap between rich and poor regions led to claims of unfair treatment by political representatives from less well-off areas. Paradoxically, these cries not only came from activists in rural regions, but also from within urban centres, like the inner city of Dublin. These issues were crystallised in the regionalisation debate of the mid-1990s. Due to the success of the economy, Ireland as a whole no longer qualified for maximum EU Structural funding. The country therefore had to be sub-divided regionally in order to increase its share.

Responding to its precarious position as a minority administration, the Fianna Fáil and Progressive Democrat coalition government initially proposed to Brussels that in addition to the Border, Midlands and West, the so-called BMW region, both the counties of Clare in the Mid-West and Kerry in the South-West should qualify for maximum funding. This was met with heated debate, with representatives of counties left out, such as Carlow and Tipperary, protesting that they should also have been included, while representatives of poor urban areas were claiming that their areas had been completely excluded from such assistance. In the end, the EU Commission decided that the BMW would qualify for full funding, with Dublin/Mid-East, the South-East, Mid-West and South-West, the so-called South and East region getting a lower level of assistance.

---

[1] These are Regional Authority boundaries. See at the end of this chapter Figure 1.1 for a map and Table 1.1 for definitions of the Regional Authority areas.

By 2000 it became clear that the "regional problem" was on the national agenda. In launching its National Development Plan: 2000-2006, the government promoted the objective of balanced regional development to become one of the three headline national objectives, alongside the traditional targets of maintaining growth and employment. This was a response to the increasing regional inequality being observed, but also to the emergence of local pockets of poverty in urban areas. It was followed in 2002 by the launch of the National Spatial Strategy 2002-2020, which was to be a more detailed blueprint for balanced regional development. This identified an urban hierarchy of gateways, hubs and smaller towns and villages. However, predictably, the strategy met with protests from towns that were not named as gateways and hubs.

At the same time as these developments were unfolding, a debate was taking place about the causes of the Celtic Tiger and the prospects for sustaining it. It became clear that the growth rates achieved were related to impressive performances by mostly US-owned multinational companies in high-technology sectors such as computers, electronics and pharmaceuticals. While the US economic boom and the freeing up of EU trade facilitated the performance of these companies, there was also a widespread belief that domestic factors played a role. Thus, the availability of young, well-educated English-speaking workers and the use of appropriate public policies in areas such as corporation tax, education and the public finances were also deemed to be important.

It became clear as the decade wore on, however, that in order to sustain the Celtic Tiger in the face of near full employment and rising wages, we would have to enable internationally competitive Irish, as well as foreign-owned, companies to produce high value-added products and services from Ireland. This can only be achieved by encouraging the location in the country of the key functions of innovation, such as research and development. Thus, the slogan of the industrial development agencies and the Tánaiste and Minister for Enterprise and Employment, Ms Mary Harney, has become that Ireland must "move up the value chain".

For much of the 1990s, the perspective taken in commentaries on the national economy was of "Ireland Incorporated", with relatively little attention being paid to regions within the country. Indeed, one of the few references to regions was to Ireland as a region of Europe, or more recently perhaps, as the 51st state in Europe (Doyle, Gallagher and O'Leary, 2000). As the decade progressed, however, and as Dublin/Mid-East and South-West pulled way from the rest, suggestions started to surface that their success was due to the emergence of high-technology "clusters" in these regions. For example software and international traded services were thriving in the capital city region while the highly successful pharmaceutical companies were concentrated in Cork harbour. Thus, a view started to emerge that the strength of the industries, especially in the Dublin region, was due to the emergence of agglomeration economies. In official circles, this view is present in the National Spatial Strategy 2002-2020, where it is asserted that urban centres thrived during the Celtic Tiger due to regional specialisation. However, such a view should be seen in the context of an increasingly polarised regional debate that had emerged, with the growing gap between rich and poor regions.

While the issue of regional specialisation and clusters were entering the agenda in late 1990s, it was already obvious a deficit in our transportation infrastructure was emerging, particularly in and around Dublin. Greater wealth during the Celtic Tiger boom resulted in increasing numbers of vehicles on our roads, with, for example, the number of new cars mushrooming from 82,000 to 225,000 between 1995 and 2000. At the same time, due to supply constraints, house prices were increasing sharply.

In the absence of viable public transport alternatives, the result has been severe pressure on an already inadequate road system with ever-increasing numbers of vehicles commuting ever-increasing distances. The effect was the economy of the Dublin area increasing to include not just the surrounding Mid-East counties, but also extending to parts of the South-East, the Midlands and the Border. With traffic congestion in the capital continuing to escalate, commuting times have increased alarmingly. These problems are also being experienced, albeit to a lesser degree, in the country's other urban centres.

Given that Ireland is a peripheral nation with a large reliance on international travel and trade, the country's air and port infrastructure also faced increasing constraints as the decade wore on. Both Dublin and Cork airports witnessed massive growth in passengers, averaging round 10 per cent annually since 1992. Similarly, Dublin and other ports have also witnessed substantial growth in freight.

The growing infrastructural deficit predictably resulted in pressing requirements for new investment programmes on roads, airports and ports. In addition, other economic infrastructure, such as energy, communications, water and waste services, also required urgent attention. As the main provider of infrastructure this has placed significant pressure on the public sector to fund the increased investment. As the decade progressed, claims of inertia in the public sector led to calls for private sector involvement. Thus, for example, there were proposals for the much-needed new terminal at Dublin Airport from a number of prominent private interests. This debate has heightened in the last three years, as the roar of the Celtic Tiger faded, resulting in restrictions in government expenditure.

Added to these issues, are growing concerns about the integrity of our public institutions, especially in relation to planning laws. The numerous tribunals investigating alleged corruption by politicians and public servants in the rezoning of lands has served to undermine public confidence in local authorities not just in Dublin, but also around the country. In these circumstances it is not surprising that doubt has been cast on the capability of these institutions to deal with the growing infrastructural deficit.

A NEW AGENDA FOR REGIONAL DEVELOPMENT

The above outline of the emerging regional debate identifies the three key issues that are central in this book. These are the appropriate stance of regional policy, the importance of innovation for future growth and the need to address the growing infrastructural deficit. The public debate on these issues has lacked an economics perspective, as other viewpoints, especially that of social equity, have tended to dominate. This is exemplified by the discussion on regional policy, which has been viewed as a means of bringing about spatial equity through balanced regional development. This is the position, not just of the many lobbyists but also of the government, as elaborated in the National Spatial Strategy.

Indeed, it almost seems as if the economics profession is an interloper in this debate, which has been traditionally dominated by social and political perspectives. This is perhaps understandable, as it was only during the 1990s that it became evident that for the first time in its history, the Irish economy was faced with serious regional problems which have the potential of undermining future national prosperity. It might also partly explain why heretofore only a handful of professional economists took an interest in Irish regional issues.

It is now timely for the increasing number of economists working on Irish regional issues to set a new agenda for thinking about these issues. This book is the first to provide a comprehensive analysis of the problems and opportunities facing Irish regions at the beginning of the new millennium and to analyse, from an economics perspective, the key drivers of Irish regional development. As the first book to critically evaluate the recently launched National Spatial Strategy, it clearly reveals how future national economic prosperity depends on suitable policies being designed for each of the regions. In doing so it uncovers some of the stark choices involved in using regional policies to bring about greater spatial equity as opposed to increased national prosperity.

The book is an edited volume, in which internationally respected, mostly Irish-based, economists present up-to-date and accessible analyses of the key areas in Irish regional development. These are the regional policy dilemma, the issue of regional growth and innovation and the infrastructural deficit. Based on the recent literature in these fields, the contributions in the book draw from original surveys and case studies of Irish regions, as well as the experiences of other EU countries, to provide thought-provoking and insightful analyses of these issues.

The book is based on the proceedings of a very successful symposium, "A New Agenda for Irish Regional Development", held in UCC in September 2002. Over 100 participants, mostly consisting of Irish regional analysts and policymakers, attended this event, which was chaired by John O'Brien, Special Advisor to the Tánaiste and Minister for Enterprise and Employment, Ms Mary Harney. The symposium was widely covered in the national print media at the time. Its success demonstrates that there is a strong interest for thought-provoking and accessible analyses of regional issues in Ireland.

THE CONTRIBUTIONS IN THE BOOK

The book is divided into three parts, dealing with the key issues of regional policy, innovation and infrastructure. Part 1 begins with a chapter in which I present a critical evaluation of Irish regional policy. This chapter is critical of the National Development Plan: 2000-06 and the National Spatial Strategy: 2002-20. I show that the failure of government to realise that growth in Ireland depends, more than ever before, on the performance of regions outside Dublin, may jeopardise national prosperity over the next 20 years. I argue that the existing goals of maintaining national growth and competitiveness and ensuring balanced regional development are incompatible and should be replaced by a single objective, that of improved regional growth and competitiveness, with Regional Authorities being given a strengthened role in developing strategies for regional competitiveness.

Chapters 3 and 4 offer a European perspective. Chapter 3 is by Mike Danson, who is chairman of the internationally recognised Regional Studies Association. Based on his extensive work on Regional Development Agencies (RDAs) and economic development in Europe and Scotland in particular, Mike argues that in contrast to the historic tendency towards competition for foreign direct investment between the Celtic nations, the enlargement and deepening of the EU is exacerbating their shared peripherality, with the result that for the first time in the new millennium, common cause and partnership across these nations and between their regions may be more appropriate in the future. This is followed in Chapter 4 by John Dewhurst, who is a leading figure in these islands in the Regional Science Association International. John shows, based on evidence from

Great Britain, that a national blueprint for a regional policy might not perform well, due to the difficulty of "picking winners" when choosing industrial sectors or clusters of sectors for support. As a result he argues that Irish regions should focus on policies tailored to their own particular circumstances, rather than adopting a more general simplistic strategy.

Part 2 begins with Edgar Morgenroth of the ESRI in Dublin, who sets the scene in Chapter 5 by outlining the recent advances in economic growth theory and new economic geography. Instead of relying on often-simplistic descriptive analysis, Edgar argues that Irish policymakers should use these theories to improve their understanding of the mechanisms that determine the growth and location of Irish economic activity. This is followed in Chapter 6 by Stephen Roper (who recently took the Chair of Innovation at Aston University in the UK having formerly worked in the Northern Ireland Economic Research Centre, Belfast) and his colleagues, who present an in-depth analysis on the question of public support for research and development (R&D) centres in less favoured regions. They argue, based on an extensive investigation of the international literature, that it is difficult for these regions to appropriate many of the benefits from R&D activity. From an Irish perspective, this has the very important implication that policymakers should undertake detailed evaluations before committing public funding to such initiatives.

This is followed in Chapter 7 by Bernadette Andreosso-O'Callaghan, from the University of Limerick, and her colleagues who present very interesting survey results which show that the major disparities in knowledge creation capability are not between the BMW region and the South and East region but within these two broad regions. This result has significant implications for Irish policymakers. Part 2 concludes with Rachel Hilliard, of NUI Galway, and David Jacobson, of Dublin City University, presenting interesting evidence on environmental regulation in the pharmaceutical industry. They argue that the concentration of pharmaceutical firms in the Cork area may have encouraged the upgrading of environmental competence in these firms, in the regulators and in other supporting institutions in that region.

Part 3 of the book deals with the issue of the transport infra-structure deficit. It begins in Chapter 9 with Aisling Reynolds-Feighan, who is an internationally respected transport econo-mist, working in University College Dublin. Aisling shows that despite substantial investment in the past and, taking into ac-count future spending as part of the current National Develop-ment Plan, infrastructure capacity in Ireland will be exceeded in the next 5 to 10 years. She goes on to argue that Irish trans-port policy requires long-run planning in order to improve the efficiency of Ireland's regional economies. In Chapter 10 Ella Kavanagh and her colleagues from UCC measure the impact of Cork Airport on the South-West region. We propose that for Cork Airport to play its key role as an infrastructural facility in the region, the recently announced break-up of Aer Rianta should be carried out in such a way that key regional stake-holders are included on an independent board, thus enabling Cork Airport to develop its own strategies, including a com-mercial strategy to exploit non-aeronautical sources of reve-nue. Finally, in Chapter 11 Michael Keane, from NUI Galway, criticises the *ad hoc* approaches by policymakers to the crucial issue of measuring functional economic areas in Irish regions. Using census data for County Galway he shows how methods from the regional science literature are useful in understanding these functional areas.

Figure 1.1: Regional Authority Areas

Table 1.1: Definition of Regional Authority Areas

Regions	Counties
Border	Cavan, Donegal, Leitrim, Louth, Monaghan and Sligo.
Dublin/Mid-East	Dublin, Kildare, Meath and Wicklow.
Midlands	Laois, Longford, Offaly and Westmeath.
Mid-West	Limerick, Clare and Tipperary North Riding.
South-East	Waterford, Carlow, Kilkenny, Wexford and Tipperary South Riding.
South-West	Cork and Kerry.
West	Galway, Mayo and Roscommon.

References

Doyle, E., Gallagher, L. and O'Leary, E. (2000), *The Celtic Tiger: The 51st State in Europe.* Paper prepared for Professor Michael Porter, Harvard Business School, for a presentation by Michael Porter in University College Cork on 25th October.

National Development Plan 2000-2006 (2000), Dublin: Stationery Office.

National Spatial Strategy for Ireland 2002-2020: People, Places and Potential (2002), Dublin: Stationery Office.

O'Leary, E. (2002/03), "Sources of Regional Divergence in the Celtic Tiger: Policy Responses". Paper Presented to a Meeting of the Statistical and Social Inquiry Society of Ireland, ESRI, Dublin, 7th November 2002. Forthcoming in *Journal of the Statistical and Social Inquiry Society of Ireland.*

PART 1

Ireland's Regional Policy Dilemma

Chapter 2

A CRITICAL EVALUATION OF IRISH REGIONAL POLICY

Eoin O'Leary

INTRODUCTION

At the beginning of the new millennium, regional issues are on the policy agenda in the Republic of Ireland. Policymakers are faced with the dilemma of achieving the twin objectives of maintaining the very strong national performance of the economy during the 1990s, which was characterised as the "Celtic Tiger" boom, while simultaneously, bringing about convergence of living standards between Irish regions.

By the end of the 1990s strong divergence in regional living standards had emerged, resulting in higher factor costs and infrastructure bottlenecks, especially in the Dublin region. The government response has been to insert "balanced regional development" as a key long-term objective in the National Development Plan: 2000-2006 and to develop the National Spatial Strategy 2002-2020.

This chapter presents a critical evaluation of Irish regional policy. It asks whether current policy will deliver the goals of balanced regional development and improving national growth and competitiveness. It begins by briefly reviewing the causes of the Celtic Tiger boom of the 1990s, with particular reference to the role of Irish regions. The next section provides an outline of the existing regional policies, while the following section presents an assessment of these policies in the context of the drivers of future Irish growth and competitiveness. The final section concludes with recommendations for change.

THE ROLE OF THE REGIONS IN THE "CELTIC TIGER" BOOM

Although much has been written about the "Celtic Tiger boom", there is no clear consensus about its causes. This section begins by outlining the different explanations of the boom. It then proceeds to consider the role played by Irish regions.

There is agreement among commentators that the most remarkable feature of the Celtic Tiger was the extraordinary growth in employment. For example, Kennedy (2000/2001) shows that growth in GDP per capita during the 1990s was accounted for by a rise in the employment-population ratio, due to improvements in the employment, participation and age-dependency rates. This rise has been referred to as the "demographic dividend". Kennedy shows that during the period no acceleration occurred in labour productivity growth, which has averaged at 3.5 per cent per annum for the last five decades. He argues that the US boom and increased penetration by Irish exports on EU markets were important causes of the boom. Ireland was able to win an increasing share of US foreign direct investments in Europe. This was due to such factors as favourable corporation tax rates, a plentiful supply of young well-educated English-speaking workers, and improvements in human capital and physical infrastructure funded by EU Structural Funds, and sound public finances. However, Kennedy concludes that we lack a convincing analysis on the timing and relative importance of these factors.

Ó Gráda (2002) argues that the Irish economy exhibited delayed convergence during the late 1980s and 1990s. The progress during this period should, in accordance with standard growth theory, have been made in earlier decades, when Ireland stood out for its failure, compared to other similarly positioned countries like Italy, to catch up on more advanced economies. It is argued that conditions for recovery were right beginning in the mid-1980s due to the coincidence of the same factors as identified by Kennedy. However, as Kennedy argues, it is not clear why it took so long for some of these factors like, for example, the growth of human capital or the restoration in public finances, to exert such a positive effect (2000/01).

Barry (2002) prefers the regional boom perspective, originally proposed for Ireland by Krugman (1997). This perspective treats Ireland as a regional economy. It suggests that the performance of Ireland's export base is the key. According to this explanation, the abundance of foreign direct investment from the late 1980s facilitated the rapid growth that followed. This echoes Kennedy's emphasis on the importance of the US boom and improved performance of Irish exports (2000/01).

Most commentators agree that the economy currently faces a number of threats, some of which are already exerting an influence. These include a breakdown in social partnership, a slowdown in US growth, and pressures from enlargement of the EU. Gallagher, Doyle and O'Leary (2002) argue that factors such as the "demographic dividend", which helped to create the Celtic Tiger, were once-off and will not sustain growth at similar rates in the future. They point to weaknesses in the micro-foundations of Irish competitiveness to be addressed. These include the appearance of a strong self-reinforcing process of innovation in Irish-based industry, the emergence of vibrant clusters of related and supporting industries and removing anti-competitive practices in the sheltered sectors. These weaknesses must be addressed if productivity growth, which is the key to future national prosperity, is to continue to grow at around 3.5 per cent per annum.

Given that a regional "problem" had emerged by the end of the 1990s, as evidenced by higher factor costs and infrastructure bottlenecks primarily in the Dublin region, it is clearly important to understand the role of regions in the Celtic Tiger boom. Were particular Irish regions more attractive to US foreign direct investment than others? If so, why? This calls for analysis of the competitiveness of Irish regions, with particular emphasis on the role of internationally competitive industries.

Relatively little work has been done in this area.[1] However, O'Leary (2002/2003) has shown that during the 1990s regional living standards diverged strongly, driven both by the emergence of the "demographic dividend" and productivity growth. Table 2.1 shows that growth in per capita regional gross value added (GVA) was highest in the most prosperous Regional Authority (RA) areas of Dublin/Mid-East and the South-West and lowest in the South-East, the Midlands and the Border.[2] Productivity growth, as measured by regional GVA per worker, contributed 42 per cent on average to living standards growth, which was highest in the South-West and the Border. The contribution from the "demographic dividend" was 58 per cent on average, which was highest in the Midlands, Dublin/Mid-East and the South-East.

Table 2.1: Decomposition of Living Standards Growth in Irish Regional Authority Areas: 1993–99 (% p.a.)

	Living Standards (GVA per capita)	Productivity (GVA per worker)	"Demographic Dividend" (employment per capita)
Border	+6.6	+3.1	+3.5
Midlands	+6.2	+2.1	+4.1
West	+7.3	+3.2	+4.1
Dublin/Mid-East	+8.3	+3.1	+5.2
Mid-West	+7.3	+2.8	+4.5
South-East	+5.3	+2.0	+3.3
South-West	+8.5	+4.7	+3.8
State	+7.7	+3.3	+3.4

Source: O'Leary 2002/03.

---

[1] Boyle, McCarthy and Walsh, 1998/9; Bradley and Morgenroth, 1999; and O'Leary, 1999; 2001a; 2001b; 2002/2003 and 2003 are examples.

[2] See, on page 11, Figure 1.1 for map and Table 1.1 for definitions of the RA regions.

O'Leary (2002/2003) proceeds to show that overall productivity divergence was driven from the manufacturing sector. Dublin/ Mid-East, the Mid-West and the South-West were the regions with highest manufacturing productivity growth, with the Border, the South-East and the Midlands being the lowest. These findings confirm that one of the chief factors explaining regional divergence during the Celtic Tiger boom was productivity growth in the internationally competitive, mostly foreign-owned multinational companies in the high-technology computer, electronics and pharmaceutical sectors concentrated in the regions with major urban centres, like Dublin, Cork and Limerick.

Given that it is predicted that the demographic dividend will only contribute 1 per cent per annum to national growth to 2010 (Duffy, Fitzgerald, Hore, Kearney and MacCoille, 2001: p. 42), it is clear that productivity growth will be the chief determinant of future Irish living standards. In order to achieve an average productivity growth rate of 3.5 per cent per annum for the rest of this decade, it is necessary that these internationally competitive industries continue to perform.

From a regional policy perspective, this involves strengthening the micro-foundations of competitiveness in the particular centres within the country in which internationally competitive industries are located, or are likely to locate. This clearly involves more than just controlling house price inflation and removing infrastructural bottlenecks in cities such as Dublin. It also crucially necessitates investment in human capital in the regions to meet the human resource requirements of these businesses, especially in relation to workers involved in research and development, development of clusters of related and supporting industries in the regions and improvements in the "quality of life" associated with living and working in the regions.

The next section provides an outline of current regional policy. This is followed by analysis of whether this policy is capable of rising to this challenge.

AN OUTLINE OF REGIONAL POLICY

Before the mid-1990s regional policy in Ireland was not regarded as particularly important. This is partly due to Ireland as a whole, as a single NUTS 2 region, qualifying for Objective 1 status for EU Structural Funds. However, it was also a by-product of the absence of any serious regional economic problem within the country. The poor performance of the economy, especially during the 1980s, meant that all Irish regions had plenty of growth potential. The emergence of a regional problem since the mid-1990s, which may constrain future national growth, has been a new challenge for policymakers. This section considers their response to this threat.

The National Development Plan: 2000-2006 (NDP)

Leading up to the NDP, which was launched in 2000, the government made a number of key regional policy decisions, mostly due to the need to fulfil EU requirements in relation to Structural Funds. In 1994 it instituted eight new Regional Authorities (RAs) corresponding to NUTS 3 regions. The statutory responsibility of RAs is to co-ordinate the regional provision of public services, to make submissions to government on regional investment priorities and to review the implementation of Structural Funds. Directives were also given to all public sector agencies to, as far as is practicable, adopt the new RA boundaries in implementing the plan. Membership of the RAs comprises elected public representatives, nominated by each of the constituent Local Authorities in each region.

In 1995, five of Ireland's RAs — Dublin, Mid-East, Mid-West, South-East and South-West — surpassed the limit for Objective 1 qualification. During lengthy negotiations with the EU, the government unsuccessfully attempted to have parts of the Mid-West and South-West (i.e. counties Clare and Kerry respectively) remain as Objective 1 regions. The outcome was that for the current round, for the first time, Ireland is treated as two NUTS 2 regions. The Border, Midlands and West (BMW) region qualifies as Objective 1, with the remaining five regions, known as the South & East (S&E) region, qualifying as Objective 1 in Transition. The government instituted two new Regional Assemblies in 1999 corresponding to the BMW and S&E regions. The functions of the assemblies are similar to those of RAs.

To reflect the emerging regional problem, the NDP included, for the first time, balanced regional development as a fundamental national objective, along with the long-standing objectives of maintaining growth and employment. This is a significant development. The NDP is to be executed through four national operational programmes and two regional operational programmes, managed by the BMW and S&E Regional Assemblies. The regional development objectives of the NDP are to pursue balanced regional development, both between and within each NUTS 2 region, to address urban bottlenecks in the S&E region and to promote social inclusion in both regions. This latter objective refers to the presence of local pockets of poverty mostly in urban areas.

Table 2.2 shows that the NDP is a major development programme, with planned spending of the order of €47 billion, or approximately 10 per cent of GNP annually during its lifetime. Under the plan the BMW region is to receive 30 per cent of total funding. In per capita terms this represents 15 per cent more than the national average, with the S&E receiving 5 per cent less. The most important programmes are on infrastructure[3] and human resources, which together account for 83 per cent of spending. No details are provided in the plan on the distribution of funding by programme to the RA regions.

Turning to the regional development section of the NDP, although a clear role for urban centres or gateways in regional development is identified, it is also envisaged that medium-sized towns, or development hubs, and even smaller towns and villages will be the focus of regional policy. The key emphasis is "spreading the benefits of national economic development more widely across the regions" (NDP, 2000: p. 44). As part of the NDP, the government mandated the Department of the Environment and Local Government to prepare a more detailed blueprint for balanced regional development through the National Spatial Strategy.

---

[3] See Aisling Reynolds-Feighan's contribution in Chapter 9 of this volume for a discussion on the planned investment in transport infrastructure.

Table 2.2: National Development Plan 2000-2006: Proposed Overall and Per Capita Spending in BMW and S&E Regions by Programme

Overall Spending (€ million)	State	BMW	%	S&E	%
Economic & Social Infrastructure	26,259	7,895	30	18,703	70
Employment & Human Resources	12,562	3,595	29	8,967	71
Productive Sector	6,582	2,529	38	4,053	62
Social Inclusion	1,344	281	21	1,063	79
Total	*47,085*	*14,300*	*30*	*32,786*	*70*
Per Capita Spending (€000)	**State**	**BMW**	**%**	**S&E**	**%**
Economic & Social Infrastructure	7,102	7,998	113	6,781	95
Employment & Human Resources	3,354	3,642	109	3,251	97
Productive Sector	1,758	2,562	146	1,470	84
Social Inclusion	359	285	79	385	107
Total	*12,573*	*14,488*	*115*	*11,888*	*95*

Source: NDP, 2000.

The National Spatial Strategy 2002-2020 (NSS)

The NSS was designed in accordance with the guiding principles of maintaining economic competitiveness (NDP, 2000: p. 45). Preparation for the NSS began in May 2000. A process was undertaken, involving commissioning a range of research studies, engaging in public consultation through regional road shows and developing policy papers before adoption. A considerable amount of effort has been devoted to the NSS. It was launched in November 2002.

The approach taken by the NSS to achieve balanced regional development involves "developing the full potential of each area to contribute to the optimal performance of the State as a whole — economically, socially and environmentally" (NSS, 2002: p. 11). Much of the country's economic success is attributed to the Greater Dublin Area.[4] Balanced regional development is to be achieved by other regions emulating the success of this area.

---

[4] The Dublin/Mid-East region.

The policy focus is an urban hierarchy, consisting of gateways, hubs and other towns and villages. The gateways are presented in Figure 2.1. They are defined as the national engines of growth and are characterised as having a large urban population, with large clusters of national/international scale enterprises and city levels of services and infrastructure in areas such as education, health, recreation, transport, communications and environment (NSS, 2002: p. 40). In addition to the existing urban centres in Dublin, Cork, Limerick, Galway and Waterford, four new potential gateways are selected. These are:

- Letterkenny in the north-west of the Border, which is close to Derry, Northern Ireland's second largest city

- Dundalk in the east of the Border, which is on the Dublin-Belfast corridor

- Sligo in the West, and

- A triangular gateway in the Midlands consisting of Athlone, Mullingar and Tullamore.

The rationale for the selection of the new potential gateways is either to build links with existing urban centres or to rectify a perceived weakness in the urban structure of a region. The former applies to Letterkenny and Dundalk, but also to the triangular gateway in the Midlands, where the objective is to build links with Dublin and Galway. The selection of Sligo and Letterkenny is also attributed to weakness in the urban structure of the Border region (NSS, 2002: pp. 41-8).

Hubs, which are also presented in Figure 2.1, are to support gateways. These are characterised as having a significant urban population, with a mix of businesses serving regional/national/international markets and adequate levels of services and infrastructure in areas such as education, health, recreation, transport, communications and environment (NSS, 2002: p. 40). A total of nine hubs are identified. These are:

- Wexford and Kilkenny in the South-East

- Mallow and a linked hub, Tralee/Killarney in the South-West

- Ennis in the Mid-West

- Monaghan and Cavan in the Border, and

- Tuam and a linked hub, Castlebar/Ballina in the West.

The rationale for the selection of these towns as hubs is either their location on transport corridors between gateways or in the cases of Tralee/Killarney and Castlebar/Ballina, to reinforce dynamic rural economies (NSS, 2002: pp. 41-8). In addition other towns, villages and rural areas are to play complementary roles to hubs and gateways.

Figure 2.1: National Spatial Strategy: 2002-2020: Proposed Gateways and Hubs

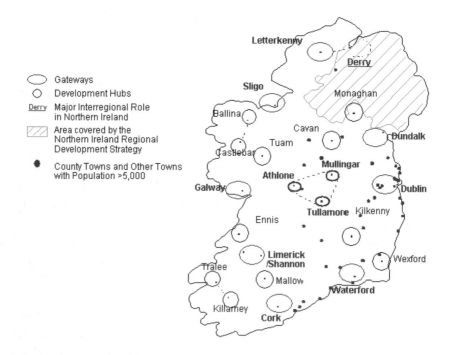

EVALUATING REGIONAL POLICY

At the end of the 1990s, the Irish government's view is that the problem of regional imbalance is more serious than in the recent past, as continuing infrastructural bottlenecks have the potential of hindering future national growth. This section presents a critical evaluation of existing regional policy. Five points arise.

First, there were significant delays in the NSS, which was to be delivered by the end of 2001. The government's reluctance to decide on the identity of new gateways and hubs may be explained by the timing of the May 2002 general election. The governing parties clearly feared incurring the wrath of local communities not selected under the NSS in advance of the election. The launch of the strategy in November 2002 resulted in predictable complaints from certain overlooked towns, like Drogheda and Portlaoise. In terms of the NDP, the delay in the NSS implies that the government has almost completed one-half of a seven-year programme, without a spatial strategy.

This shows that political expediency has delayed attempts to address the spatial problem. It seems as if by setting spending targets for each programme and for the NUTS 2 regions, when the NDP was launched in 2000, the government did not need an NSS. This raises the question: on what basis was NDP funding actually spent between and within the NUTS 2 regions for the first three years? Was the government's objective in distributing NDP funding to maximise its chances of re-election? Further evidence that political short-sightedness dominates government action in this regard is provided by the ultimately failed attempt in 1995 to re-negotiate with the EU to have parts of the Mid-West and South-West remain as Objective 1 regions. The objective was to placate a small number of independent members of parliament whose vote the government needed to stay in power at the time. Clearly, the NSS should have been prepared in advance of the NDP. By failing to do so a significant cost may already have been incurred, as improvements in long-term national competitiveness may have already been compromised.

Second, even though balanced regional development has emerged in the NDP: 2000-2006 as a fundamental objective alongside maintaining national growth and competitiveness, the arrangements instituted for implementing regional policy reveal the latter as the primary economic objective of government. Regional issues are seen to arise in the context of achieving regional balance by distributing the benefits of national growth. This objective has been coupled with other distributional objectives, such as social inclusion. In terms of economic policy, regional policy is given low priority, being managed by the Department of the Environment and Local Government and not by the main economic ministries. The NSS is weak on implementation as it does not contain specific measures, but rather requires government departments to integrate the NSS into their policies (Morgenroth, 2003). It is significant that the existing regional policy stance is broadly similar to that of the two previous plans (National Development Plan, 1994 and 1989), when a regional "problem" was not a threat. Regional policy was and continues to be regarded as distributive rather than as a key influence on economic growth. This shows that there is little realisation among national political decision makers of the centrality of regions for future national competitiveness. Their mindset ignores Krugman's compelling argument that national competitiveness is a misleading term and that it is not countries that are competitive but firms located in them (1994).

Third, the roles of RAs and the new regional assemblies in monitoring and evaluating public spending in their regions has been very limited as government departments continue to manage NDP programmes. For the current NDP, even though two new regional operational programmes were introduced, to be monitored by the new Regional Assemblies, closer inspection reveals that these programmes are themselves sub-divided into the four national programmes. Thus, de facto programme management is carried out by government departments. Both the RAs and the new Regional Assemblies have had difficulties in fulfilling their statutory responsibilities. For example, mid-way into the NDP, neither body has detailed information on the amount of funding drawn down under each of the operational programmes that is necessary for them to co-ordinate the provision of public services in their areas. It seems as if the introduction of new regional operational programmes were presented primarily to satisfy EU requirements emanating from Brussels.

The limited role played by RAs was also a feature of the previous development plan. Fitzpatrick and Associates, in their mid-term evaluation of the 1994-99 Community Support Framework, found that there was a "system failure" (1997: p. xv) in the review of its implementation by RAs. This was due to RAs being under-resourced, with limited expertise to scrutinise the complex information provided by the large number of government departments and agencies involved, as well as being served by unwieldy committees, with a preponderance of politicians. Further practical difficulties faced by RAs in fulfilling their roles is evidenced by the finding that in 2001 there were up to thirty public sector strategies in existence using different regional boundaries (Association of Irish Regions, 2001).

Fourth, regional and local government have played minor roles in Irish economic policy formulation. Economic policy is set by central government in Dublin, mainly through the Department of Finance, where the traditional emphasis has been on national competitiveness. Dublin, as the capital city, plays a very dominant role in shaping policy and public opinion (Byrne, 2001). Ireland's centralised state has failed to empower regional actors. According to Breathnach, "lack of local government reform and decentralisation of powers and competences will inevitably compromise the ability of the regions to develop themselves from within and create self-sustaining forms of dynamism" (2002: p. 3).

Regional political representatives typically favour short-term local interests at the expense of long-term regional growth. Thus, for example, the typical response to the closure of a multinational branch plant based in a small Irish town is usually for local politicians to exert pressure to institute a national task force to look for a replacement industry. The extent to which the industry involved is or is likely to be internationally competitive and whether it plays a role in long-term strategic planning of a region is usually ignored in the local debate. The question of whether it might be preferable to expend resources in the urban centre of the region in which the town is located, especially if this is in another county, often fails to be addressed due to local or county political considerations.

If these strategic questions were addressed, it might be realised that regional growth in both productivity and living standards might be higher if, for example, a local workforce is retrained for the internationally competitive industry based in or near the major urban centre of the region. Every town in a region does not require its own industry. Indeed, it might be preferable, from a quality of life perspective, for individuals to live in towns or villages without major industries, and, assuming adequate transport infrastructure and services, to commute to work in or near urban centres. Thus, although intra-regional productivity differences would be marked in this scenario, intra-regional differences in living standards would be more equal, as a result of commuting patterns. This phenomenon is already observed in Dublin and the Mid-East, the latter of which partially operates as a commuting area for the capital. In 1999, even though labour productivity in Dublin was 44 per cent greater than the Mid-East, living standards, as measured by per capita household primary income (that is before tax and welfare benefits), was only 17 per cent greater (CSO, 2002). In this way, city conurbations could host industry with outlying towns and villages in a region being earmarked as potential centres of high quality residential housing with appropriate public and private services.

The weaknesses in local and regional government are also clearly evident in the development strategies proposed by the NUTS 2 regions in the preparation of the NSS. The growth strategies proposed fail to make the necessary trade-offs in the selection of growth centres. This partly stems from their being required to pursue objectives such as social exclusion and rural viability as well as regional competitiveness. Thus, similar to the NDP, although a focused spatial policy is advocated, smaller towns and villages also have a role to play, in addition to the main centres. The selection of the main growth centres seems to be based on political rather than economic considerations. For example, for the BMW region the basis for selecting Sligo and Athlone as centres is that they "fill the gaps in the North-West and the Midlands" (Fitzpatrick and Associates, 1999, p. 67). This weakness also arises due to the roles played by locally elected representatives on the committees responsible for designing strategies. There is a conspicuous lack of involvement on these committees by locally based internationally competitive industry in formulating these strategies. Failure to empower the key regional actors will hinder future competitiveness.

Fifth, the lack of regional economic research has severely constrained attempts to develop meaningful strategies for regional competitiveness. The NSS can be criticised for its under-use of regional economic analysis. Only one of the studies commissioned for the NSS was economic, and this was more descriptive than analytical. Data constraints have been a factor limiting analytical work. However, the lack of interest in regional issues by the economics profession based in Ireland has also played a role. The result has been an almost complete absence of empirical studies drawing on a range of theoretical approaches used for other countries. (See Edgar Morgenroth's contribution in Chapter 5 and Stephen Roper at al.'s contribution in Chapter 6 of this volume for reviews.)

The net effect has been little convincing evidence in the NSS on the underlying sources of recent growth in the regions that might reveal the drivers of growth, in terms of identifying internationally competitive industries and firms and the factors giving rise to their success in each region. The rationale offered for the selection of new gateways and hubs is based exclusively on location and the availability of a critical mass of population, with associated services (NSS, 2002: pp. 149-151). For example, it is questionable whether an urban structure of sufficient scale and complexity to host internationally competitive industry could be created in the Athlone, Mullingar and Tullamore triangle or in Sligo. It should be noted that this criticism is not new as the dearth of detailed regional research was also seen as a constraint by Fitzpatrick and Associates (1997: pp. 112-118) in their mid-term evaluation of the 1994-99 Community Support Framework.

It should be emphasised finally that this chapter is not arguing that growth and competitiveness are the only worthwhile objectives. Redistribution may also be worthwhile. The point is that the objectives of growth and distribution should be decoupled. It should be noted however, that the tax and welfare systems already have a redistributive effect on regional household incomes. For example, in 1999 the coefficient of variation of disposable income per capita was 10.6 per cent for Irish regions compared to 15.3 per cent for primary income per capita (CSO, 2002). Thus, if the objective is that income distribution should be more equitable across regions, this might be achieved through taxation and welfare changes. In addition, redistributional objectives such as rural development and social inclusion could be pursued through separate programmes. These might be more successful, as there would be less mixing of targets and instruments, which characterises the present approach.

THE WAY FORWARD

In critically evaluating Irish regional policy, this chapter has argued that current policy is likely to jeopardise future national growth. The problem stems from the failure to recognise that, for Ireland in the early decades of the new millennium, continued national growth and competitiveness requires appropriate policies at a regional level. Despite the elevation of regional balance as a fundamental objective, there seems to be little realisation that future national growth will depend more than ever before on growth in regions.

There is a distinct possibility that the objectives of balanced regional development and improved national growth and competitiveness may not be simultaneously achievable. According to O'Leary (2002/03), balanced regional development over the next two decades depends on higher productivity growth in internationally traded sectors, such as manufacturing and services, for relatively low productivity regions, such as the Border, the Midlands, the West and the South-East. The likelihood of this occurring depends on the factors shaping productivity in these regions and their more prosperous neighbours. The issues involved may be considered for the two scenarios identified in Table 2.3.

Table 2.3: Balanced Regional Development and Regional Growth Scenarios

	"Rich" Regions	"Poor" Regions
1st Scenario: Regional Convergence or Balanced Regional Development	Urban Diseconomies Dominate	Exploit Catch-Up Potential
2nd Scenario: Regional Divergence or Unbalanced Regional Development	Agglomeration Economies Dominate	Failure to Catch-up

The first involves balanced regional development. It envisages that urban diseconomies in the form of congestion and higher factor costs in Dublin and to a lesser extent in Cork and Limerick, dominate over the next number of decades. If these inhibit growth in the more prosperous regions, and if the less prosperous regions are able to exploit their catch-up potential, then balanced regional development or regional convergence would be the outcome. This view finds support in the Williamson (1965, cited in Keane, 2002) hypothesis, which suggests that as countries catch up regional disparities may initially increase, due to the emergence of growth poles, but may subsequently lessen as urban diseconomies emerge. A second scenario envisages unbalanced regional development. This might occur if agglomeration economies in urban centres strengthen and outweigh the emerging diseconomies and if poorer regions fail to exploit their catch-up potential. This view is supported by new growth theory, which generally predicts divergence. The absence of empirical economic research on these competing hypotheses in the Irish case, which is only partly explained by lack of data, severely inhibits our capability to assess these or other scenarios at this time.

What is clear, however, is that neither of these scenarios would deliver the greatest improvement in national growth and competitiveness. From a national perspective, the ideal outcome would be for agglomerate economies to dominate in "rich" regions and for the "poor" regions to exploit their catch-up potential. If this is achieved, the result may be either balanced or unbalanced regional development, depending on the relative performance of "rich" and "poor" regions.

There is strong evidence to suggest, based on the lack of both urgency and priority given by national government to addressing the emerging "regional problem", that national growth and competitiveness is, as it always has been, the most important national policy objective. Thus, it might be argued that the pursuit of balanced regional development would never be allowed to undermine national prosperity. However, this makes the mistake of ignoring the fact that at the current stage of development of the country, the issues of national and regional growth and competitiveness are inter-dependent. The failure of national policymakers to understand that regional competitiveness is the key to future national competitiveness has been an important and potentially damaging shortcoming. The result may paradoxically be the worst of both worlds, with urban diseconomies dominating in the "rich" regions and the "poor" regions failing to catch up due, at least in part, to the failure of regional policy to deliver.

This leads to the main recommendation of this chapter, which is that the existing primary policy goal of maintaining national growth and competitiveness, and the secondary goal of balanced regional development, should be replaced by a single objective, that of improved regional growth and competitiveness. This requires that three policy initiatives are introduced as a matter of urgency. The first is that the existing Regional Authority boundaries should be assessed in order to determine whether they are functional economic areas. This requires detailed economic research using up-to-date data, including population levels and commuting flows from the 2002 Census of Population.

Given the size of the country, it is probably only feasible to think of perhaps seven regions. These could be loosely based on existing RA boundaries, with minor adjustments being made. For example, Dublin and the Mid-East could form one region, due to the large amount of inter-regional commuting. Indeed, this seems to be the view already taken in the NSS, as this region is referred to as the Greater Dublin Area. The Midlands does not currently host a city. As a result it might be preferable to amalgamate this region into adjoining regions. The Border could be divided into two distinct regions. The North-East, and especially Louth, is linked to the Dublin-Belfast corridor and hosts internationally competitive manufacturing industry (Bradley and Morgenroth, 1999). The North-West is not as industrialised and is connected to Derry and Enniskillen.[5] In addition, county boundaries should not be regarded as untouchable. For example, North Kerry could be re-designated to the Mid-West, as it is part of the Shannon Development area.

---

[5] In the old regional development organisations used up to the mid-1980s, the Border region was divided into the North-East and the North-West.

The key point is that decisions should be based on up-to-date data and detailed economic analysis. (See Michael Keane's contribution in Chapter 11 of this volume for an example of a regional science method that can be used.) Once decided upon directives should be given to all public sector entities, at national, regional and local levels, to adopt the new boundaries.

Second, within each functional area, RAs should be charged with developing strategies for regional competitiveness. RAs should be strengthened to fulfil this role. There is no need to launch new agencies, as existing structures are adequate. The primary objective should be to foster an environment in which regional growth and competitiveness are improved. The task facing each region is to identify a limited number of industries that already are, or are likely, based on compelling evidence, to become internationally competitive. RAs, along with government departments, would then play a supportive role by positively influencing the environment facing these industries, through investment in projects such as infrastructure and training that are directly matched to industry needs. This requires a close partnership between government and industry. If RAs were more closely tied to the fortunes of locally based industry, they would be ideally suited to fulfil this role.

In order to fulfil their strengthened role, RAs, would have to be adequately resourced so that they would be in a position to play a meaningful role. They would need to effectively monitor and co-ordinate the provision of public services in their regions. This may involve giving RAs statutory powers. RAs would also need to undertake, in partnership with industry, detailed strategic analysis in order to identify internationally competitive industries in the region and the factors in the regional economic environment, which help and hinder their further development of competitive advantage. These analyses would provide the basis for the design of regional development strategies. Based on these strategies, RAs would then propose policy initiatives, including investment programmes in infrastructure and training, aimed at improving productivity growth in their regions. Substantial resources would be required, in terms of staff and expertise, in order to enable RAs to fulfil these tasks. Thus, Irish regions should focus on developing policies tailored to their own particular circumstances, rather than adopting a more general simplistic top-down strategy (see John Dewhurst's contribution in Chapter 4 of this volume).

The third and final recommendation is for central and local government reform in order to serve the goal of maximising regional growth. In order to fulfil their role RAs would require full cooperation from government departments and national agencies. In order to serve the goal of improving regional rather than national growth and competitiveness, some degree of re-organisation may be required in national operations. For example, in departments concerned with infrastructure, such as Environment and Local Government and Transport, it might be necessary to institute regional divisions within these departments to work closely with each of the RAs. Similarly, agencies such as the IDA might need to re-organise regionally in order to assist RAs. Any decentralisation of government departments and agencies to the regions should be based on improving the efficiency of public services in the regions, rather than on the tokenism often associated with this issue.

Given the importance of their role, RAs should supersede local authorities as the primary sub-national authority for economic planning. Democratic accountability could be provided through direct elections. In addition, reform of existing local authorities may require the amalgamation of services previously provided by neighbouring counties in a region. The precise operational details of the institutional reform required are complex and beyond the scope of this chapter. Once formulated, each RA would present its regional strategy along with suggested policy initiatives to national government. National governments would decide on the regional distribution of development funding. Its objective should be to foster regional and therefore national growth and competitiveness. Once agreed, each RA would monitor and co-ordinate delivery. Government departments, the agencies and local authorities would then be responsible for delivering operational programmes within each region. Both national government and RAs would be accountable for outcomes. This might involve regions having increased tax-raising powers. If the outcome of pursuing regional growth strategies is an unacceptable level of regional living standards divergence, then separate national re-distributional programmes could be designed in order to secure more balanced development. (See Mike Danson's contribution in Chapter 3 of this volume for a discussion of the future roles of Regional Development Agencies in peripheral areas in Europe.)

References

Association of Irish Regions (2001), Co-ordination of Strategic Planning in Ireland: Submission to the Minister for the Environment and Local Government. Tullamore, County Offaly: Association of Irish Regions, May.

Barry, F. (2002), "The Celtic Tiger Era: Delayed Convergence or Regional Boom?" *Quarterly Economic Commentary*, Summer, 84-91.

Boyle, G, McCarthy, T. and Walsh, J. (1998/9), "Regional Income Differentials and the Issue of Regional Income Equalisation in Ireland". *Journal of the Statistical and Social Inquiry Society of Ireland*, Vol. XXVIII, No. 1, 155-211.

Bradley, J. and Morgenroth, E. (1999), "Celtic Cubs? Regional Manufacturing in Ireland". In Duffy, D., Fitzgerald, J., Kearney, I. and Smyth, D. *ESRI Medium Term Review: 1999-2005*. October, pp. 157-174.

Breathnach, P. (2002), "Regional Government: The Missing Link in the National Spatial Strategy?" Paper Presented Regional Studies Association (Irish Branch) National Conference entitled *Ireland 2020: People, Place and Space*, Bunratty, County Clare, April.

Byrne, T. (2001), "The National Development Plan and the National Spatial Strategy: Can the Objective of Balanced Regional Development be Achieved?" Paper Presented at the Annual Conference of the Association of Town Clerks of Ireland, Clonakilty, County Cork, June.

Central Statistics Office (2002), *County Incomes and Regional GDP: 1999*. Dublin: Central Statistics Office, 30th January.

Duffy, D., Fitzgerald, J., Hore, J., Kearney, I. and MacCoille, C. (2001), *ESRI Medium Term Review: 2001-2007*. Summer, No. 8.

Fitzpatrick's and Associates (1999), *Border, Midland and Western Nuts II Region: Development Strategy 2000-2006*. Dublin, April.

Fitzpatrick's and Associates (1997), *Mid-Term Evaluation of the Regional Impact of the CSF for Ireland: 1994–1999*, Dublin, February.

Gallagher, L., Doyle, E. and O'Leary, E. (2002), "Creating the Celtic Tiger and Sustaining Economic Growth: A Business Perspective". *Quarterly Economic Commentary*, Spring, 63-81.

Keane, M. (2002), "Ireland in the 1990s: The Problem of Unbalanced Regional Development". In Munley V.G., Thornton R.J. and Aronson J.R. (Editors), *The Irish Economy in Transition: Successes, Problems and Prospects*. Contemporary Studies in Economic and Financial Analysis, Vol. 85, Elsevier Science, UK, pp. 205-224.

Kennedy, K. (2000/01), "Symposium on Economic Growth in Ireland: Where has it Come, Where is it Going? Reflections on the Process of Irish Economic Growth". *Journal of the Statistical and Social Inquiry Society of Ireland*. Vol. XXX, 123-139.

Krugman, P. (1994), "Competitiveness: Does It Matter?" *Fortune*, 7th March, 71-74.

Krugman, P. (1997), "Good News from Ireland: A Geographical Perspective". In Gray, A.W., (Editor). *International Perspectives on the Irish Economy*. Indecon, Dublin, pp. 38-53.

Morgenroth, E. (2003), *An Assessment of the National Spatial Strategy*. ESRI Seminar Paper, February 13th.

National Development Plan 2000-2006 (2000), Dublin: Stationery Office.

National Development Plan 1994-1999 (1994), Dublin: Stationery Office.

National Development Plan 1989-1993 (1989), Dublin: Stationery Office.

National Spatial Strategy for Ireland, 2002-2020: People, Places and Potential (2002), Dublin: Stationery Office.

Ó Gráda, C. (2002), "Is the Celtic Tiger a Paper Tiger?" *Quarterly Economic Commentary*. Spring, 51-62.

O'Leary, E. (2003), "Aggregate and Sectoral Convergence among Irish Regions: The Roles of Structural Change: 1960-96". Forthcoming in *International Regional Science Review* [Previously in Department of Economics UCC, Working Paper Series, No. 5, 1-34, 2000].

O'Leary, E. (2002/03), "Sources of Regional Divergence in the Celtic Tiger: Policy Responses". Paper Presented to a Meeting of the Statistical and Social Inquiry Society of Ireland, ESRI, Dublin, 7th November 2002. Forthcoming in *Journal of the Statistical and Social Inquiry Society of Ireland*.

O'Leary, E. (2001a), "Regional Divergence in the Celtic Tiger: The Policy Dilemma". *Irish Banking Review*. Spring, 2-15.

O'Leary, E. (2001b), "Convergence of Living Standards among Irish Regions: The Roles of Productivity, Profit Outflows and Demography: 1960-96". *Regional Studies*. Vol. 35, No. 3, 197-205.

O'Leary, E. (1999), "Regional Income Estimates for Ireland: 1995". *Regional Studies*. Vol. 33, No. 9, 805-814.

Williamson, J.G. (1965), "Regional Inequality and the Process of National Development: A Description of the Patterns". *Economic Development and Cultural Change*. Vol. 13, 3-45.

Chapter 3

REGIONAL ECONOMIC DEVELOPMENT, AGENCIES AND COMPETITIVENESS: A EUROPEAN PERSPECTIVE

Mike Danson

INTRODUCTION

There has been much discussion over whether nations and regions tend to converge or diverge over time with regard to such indicators as incomes or GDP per head (see Dewhurst in Chapter 4 of this volume). This is not unrelated to the consideration of the scheduling of movements in such variables, with claims that national growth may be a pre-requisite to achieving higher living standards everywhere within a territory; growth in the prosperous regions may be necessary for national prosperity to expand sufficiently to raise living standards everywhere. It is thus argued that catching-up processes may indeed follow expansion of the core or the leading regions, subsequent congestion there and, ultimately, the transmission of growth forces spreading out to the periphery (Myrdal, 1958; Dunford, 2003). Concerns over short- or medium-term divergence often then are focused on perceived trade-offs between equity and efficiency (O'Leary, 2001).

As the Celtic nations face up to the challenges of EU enlargement (Bachtler, Josserand, and Michie, 2002), increased competition for foreign direct investment (Danson, Helinska-Hughes and Hughes, 2002) and a progressively integrating

European market (Phelps and Raines, 2003), so the pressures to ensure that all are benefiting, or are not suffering to too great an extent, from the opportunities these developments present are being confronted by the parallel need to promote national competitiveness (Mackay, 2003). It is within these contexts that exploration of the economic development of the Irish regions must be undertaken.

This chapter proceeds by looking at the changed circumstances facing policymakers generally in north-western Europe but specifically in Ireland and Scotland, as evidenced by the apparent proposals in the National Development Plan: 2000-2006 (2000) and National Spatial Strategy: 2002-2020 (2002) in the former and the Framework for Economic Development (Scottish Executive, 2000) and A Smart Successful Scotland (Scottish Executive, 2001) in the latter. Integral to this analysis are the economic impacts of some of the elements of peripherality within this European space. As these developments and proposals each recognise the need for strategic policy responses to the changing environment, in the third section there is some investigation of the theory underpinning the rationale for intervention, before an examination of the role for regional development agencies is reviewed in section four. These foundations are used in section five to suggest that experience across Europe provides justification for proposing particular regional development vehicles in the Irish situation, but that specific regional development agencies may not be the preferred model. The paper concludes with some observations on the need for more collaborative research and policy formation, in contrast with the tendency for competition, between the Celtic nations.

FROM KEYNESIANISM TO ENDOGENOUS GROWTH

For most of the period from the end of the Second World War to the early 1970s, the dominant feature in macroeconomic policy was the influence of Keynesian economics. This sought to fulfil four key objectives simultaneously: full employment, price stability/low inflation, growth and balance of payments equilibrium. The first of these was cited as a reason for having a strong regional policy with a need to create jobs throughout the country, with the second offering support when agglomeration economies were outweighed by congestion costs in the prospering central regions. Such an approach led, for instance, to nationalised heavy industries being used to sustain and increase effective demand in the old industrial regions of many developed nations, although the so-called automatic stabilisers inherent in the taxation and welfare systems were key in spreading growth and managing decline. In the UK, for instance, coal, steel and shipbuilding industries were employed as significant means to bolster and maintain regional economies in Scotland, Wales, Northern Ireland and the north of England up to the late 1970s (Mackay, 2003), maintaining economic activity above the rates the market would have offered left to its own devices (Anyadike-Danes et al., 2001). Promoting the economies of the "problem regions" in this way (Martin and Townroe, 1992) was not considered generally as prejudicial to national development and was supported, to a greater or lesser extent, by all governments, not least because of the positive academic evaluations of their impacts (Taylor and Wren, 1997).

By way of comparison, in West Germany, high levels of national economic growth were used to raise the living standards across the country through the application of equalisation grants between the Länder. This has been claimed as advantageous for the national economy as whole (Kellermann and Schmidt, 1997) by encouraging growth in efficient regions and transferring some of the benefits nationwide, whilst also improving the ability to address inflationary pressures in these prosperous regions through expanding capacity in lagging regions and ultimately raising national effective demand.

More recently, increasing national growth in the long term through the introduction of mechanisms to promote regional growth in poorer areas has been modified by innovations in the case of Spain. In an apparent contradiction to the forces of integration in the European economy, the Basque country and other autonomous regions have captured a greater control over taxation and spending in their territories (Moreno, 2002). This has led to radically different fiscal policies across Spain, apparently allowing different areas to grow at different rates. Objectives and instruments vary across the country, reflecting different concerns and priorities when greater weight is given to strategies derived from the bottom-up. In some ways the devolution of powers to the re-established Scottish Parliament, the Welsh and Northern Ireland Assemblies is consistent with such asymmetrical developments (Jeffery and Mawson, 2002).

Other models of devolution and decentralisation can be seen in Sweden (Jensen and Leijon, 2000), France and elsewhere (Cappellin, 1997). Indeed, in a period of greater conformity in policies and institutions across the continent, the proliferation of forms of regional governance is itself of interest and cannot be unconnected to the potential conflict between cohesion and diversity (Graham and Hart, 1999).

While these moves towards enhanced powers for lower level government have been progressing, at a time of closer economic and monetary union at the EU level, the economic underpinnings of macroeconomic policies have also been evolving. Indeed, the effective end of the Keynesian model and its replacement with an approach based on monetarism and freer market forces has been accompanied by a move to endogenous economic development. Spawning a large literature drawing from the experiences of a myriad of types of area and forms of intervention — the Third Italy, clusters and competitiveness (but see Morgenroth in Chapter 5 of this volume for a useful introduction) — the focus of policy intervention has shifted from the nation down to the region and the locality. Building the capacity of the area to embrace greater indigenous development — founded on entrepreneurship, new firm formation, business development and human capital, and the attraction of mobile inward investment — where local enterprises were hitherto restricted in number and size, have been critical elements in such regional strategies.

To assist governments and regions to achieve higher rates of indigenous growth and foreign direct investment, these strategies have relied on a range of innovations in policies and institutions. In particular, regional development agencies have often been established as the preferred vehicle to deliver change (Halkier and Danson, 1997). Thus, while the abilities of nations and regions to intervene have been curtailed by international regulations and agreements, overseen by the WTO

(World Trade Organisation) and EU (European Union) especially, new ways to compete and gain comparative advantage have been sought. The reduced flexibility in applying regional policies, in using fiscal policies to benefit individual areas, and in directing nationalised enterprises to assist old industrial areas have all followed from the subordination of all other policies to the competition, free market priority. This has led to certain regimes pursuing alternative strategies more effectively and, perhaps more importantly, more timeously than others. So, regional development agencies were introduced earlier and their significance more quickly appreciated in the Celtic nations than elsewhere under these various policy changes.

Thus the Scottish Development Agency, Welsh Development Agency and the Irish Industrial Development Authority became the models for many others across Europe and beyond in the last two decades as the promotion of indigenous development and inward investment became the dominant forms of intervention to turn around declining or stagnant growth rates. UNIDO (EURADA meeting Brussels, 2000) amongst others has recognised both the leading role of Scotland and Ireland in promoting this method of supporting economic development and the evangelic broadcasting of the success of the RDA (Danson, Halkier and Cameron, 2000).

This first mover advantage, in terms of support for regional economic development, also can be seen as the initial steps by the periphery: to address loss of competitiveness for the old industrial areas of Scotland and Wales and to build competitiveness in Ireland, within the integrating European market and the globalising economy. While the work of Porter (1990) and Krugman (1997) have focused attention more on geography in the last decade than previously, there can be little doubt that agglomeration economies have been both deepening and widening the cost advantages of the core of nations and continents than is widely recognised. The literature on clusters, industrial districts and the institutional structure and capacity of regions has grown enormously since the late 1980s, but much of this, by definition, has concentrated on what is happening within the territory. Relatively fewer analyses have been undertaken of the implications of bigger developments for the individual region.

In their assessment of the state of agglomeration economies, Parr, Hewings et al. (2002) have established that the effective market size of metropolitan regions has been increasing in North America with changes in transport costs, regulations, the knowledge sectors, and in ICT technologies especially. While congestion costs may be altering the attractiveness of core city locations differentially for different industries, the net effects of these developments since 1980 have been to make the more peripheral areas relatively disadvantaged as businesses are continuously fed and generated in the metropolitan regions (Charles, 2003; Howells, 2003). Each new technological spin to the virtuous cycles of growth and economies of scale and scope in the heartland of the region and continent inevitably leaves the more remote more disadvantaged. At best, trickle down benefits are offered to the communities and enterprises of the periphery.

These tendencies can be observed on this side of the Atlantic, with Europe shrinking in time-distance terms, but where physical barriers are significant the strength of these forces is most muted. As islands, Britain and Ireland have been less able to reap the advantages of improved transportation across the continent, with the sea acting effectively to limit the decrease in times and costs to markets. Indeed, as the Channel Tunnel has reduced this barrier to entering the south of England for competitors on mainland Europe, it can be argued that Scotland and Ireland have not been helped by this major infrastructural investment and actually face increasing competition in these "home" marketplaces.

While there are similar difficulties in southern and other northern parts of the continent presented by the sheer distance from the centre of gravity of the European markets, the poor state of roads and railways, and the vagaries of the air transport system (Reynolds-Feighan, Chapter 9, this volume), the position of Ireland and Scotland on the edge of Europe is exacerbated by the sea and by the land mass of England respectively. Both are relatively disadvantaged by their geographical location and have become more so with the physical transport infrastructure investments across the EU in recent times. According to Krugman, in discussing Ireland in particular, these negative trends are modified to an extent as trade is becoming weightless (Krugman, 1997) so that infrastructure may be less important. However, the arguments of Parr, Hewings et al. (2002) on the recent evolution of agglomeration economies and the specific traditions of foreign direct investment into the Celtic countries (Danson, Helinska-Hughes and Hughes, 2003) means that their current competitive position is being undermined and their options for growth are being limited.

Within the countries making up these islands, it is no coincidence that the highest growth regions have been focused on the capital cities, which are also all located in the east of each territory. Devolution of power and responsibilities to parliaments and assemblies in Scotland, Wales and Northern Ireland has stoked the continuing development of these capital regions centred on Edinburgh, Cardiff and Belfast respectively, while the bias of growth across the developed world towards business and corporate services has benefited these and Dublin and London also. These changes have been underpinned by the reorientation of the trade of Britain and Ireland towards the countries of the EU and the continuation of the Europeanisation of the economies of all member states.

These forces have led to further tensions within these countries as their traditional industries have declined under restructuring of sectors at the European and global levels. As these sectors have tended to be dominant in the north and west of the UK, and as depopulation has adversely affected these areas and their hinterlands in Britain and in Ireland, so disparities within each territory have been aggravated. In Scotland, for example, manufacturing occupied over 30 per cent of the workforce a generation ago, now 18 per cent are so employed, and by the end of this decade the proportion is forecast to fall to 11 per cent (Green, 2001). This decline in manufacturing has been especially notable in the rural parts of the country, while the decline in coal mining and other primary sectors has also impacted most heavily outwith the metropolitan heart of the nation. Similar effects of the completion of the single European market have been felt elsewhere, but the implications in the Celtic countries of the UK have been felt more strongly because of the more rapid decline and privatisation of the nationalised industries and by the collapse of inward investment. The position of Ireland has been somewhat different in the 1990s as FDI has increased markedly, especially from the US, with very little progress on privatisation.

Acting as production bases for American and Far East multinational enterprises (MNEs) to gain entry to the EU, the fall in foreign direct investment and the increasing attractiveness of lower cost sites in central and eastern Europe has already severely hit Scotland and Wales and is likely to affect Ireland in the future. With few sustainable supply side linkages, branch plants of these MNEs have not been embedded into the local economies, staying as isolated centres of excellence within the region (Brand, Hill, and Munday, 2000). Adopting strategies based on clusters and commercialisation (Benneworth et al, 2003) built on the presence of these plants has not been successful so that the pressures on the periphery to seek new approaches to development have been growing again.

In other moves towards growth based on endogenous factors, the longer term decline of traditional industries and the reliance on inward investors have led to further difficulties for policymakers. Thus, a truncated labour process and set of functions internal to such plants has been exaggerated by the failure to sustain and promote a viable business service sector in the regions of the UK and Ireland. Although the population of this periphery of the continent is highly qualified, the restricted labour markets of the non-metropolitan regions do not encourage those with university or college educations to stay or return home after graduating (McCann and Sheppard, 2003). The attraction of the escalator regions (Fielding, 1991) of the capital cities in their own countries, or in London, Brussels or beyond, lead to progressive losses of human capital and enterprise. As labour and skill shortages have appeared across the economies of the UK and Ireland, there has been no compensatory movement of jobs and people out to the hinterlands; rather the cost spirals in housing, labour and other markets seem to have sucked even more activity to the centre. Agglomeration economies continue to dominate these and other congestion costs, with the core regions expanding out into the country while the more rural areas increase their dependence on the low paying and low multiplier sectors of retailing, food processing and tourism. The cumulative effects of these drivers of change is to depress opportunities for entrepreneurship outwith the geographical core of the economy, as incomes and capital accumulation lag behind in the rural and old industrial areas.

There are few countervailing tendencies to match the centripetal forces acting on the Celtic countries. With high and relatively increasing transport and distance barriers to the main EU markets, Scotland and Ireland in particular are faced with a set of drivers for change at a European level which demand attention to increasing national competitiveness and jointly these mitigate against policies to address growing disparities within.

THEORIES AND EXPERIENCES

To the extent that regional disparities are a national and EU priority, and there are powerful economic and political arguments to determine that they should be (see European Employment Strategy, CEC, 2002), there is an imperative to address the implications of the changes of the last few years and the anticipated developments of the next. Until now, most interest in the UK has centred on the north-south divide (Smith, 1989; Anyadike-Danes et al, 2001) and as elsewhere on the problems of types of regions — in EU terms the Objective 2 regions with their declining traditional manufacturing industries, the Objective 5b rural areas and the laggard Objective 1 regions. With most of the country so designated, disparities within Scotland and Wales have been seen as arising from these underlying structural causes. In Ireland, with its Objective 1 recognition as a nation suffering from weak development, even this level of detail has been secondary. The evolution of the structural funds into fewer categories (Bachtler, 2002) and the loss of uniformity of support across the regions have combined to encourage a re-examination of the spatial aspects of divergence and disparity. In parallel, and arising out of the need to produce single programming documents for the sub-national regions within each of the Celtic countries, questions are also raised over who determines and who delivers strategy and policy locally.

To begin to answer these issues requires a return to the literature underpinning interventions at the level of the region.

Such discussions have been all but obscured in recent times, as the significance of the rationale for addressing market failure has become dominated by what should be done to the exclusion of where.

It is now generally accepted that there are legitimate reasons for interventions by government and governance structures and institutions in the economy on several grounds: stabilisation, distribution, allocation and growth (Musgrave, 1959; Newlands, 1999). The first two of these are held to be most effectively and efficiently delivered at the highest level possible, suggesting the nation or EU, while the latter two can be more readily delivered at the sub-national level. Building on these arguments, economists such as Armstrong (1997) and King (1984) have made the case for the region being the most appropriate level or jurisdiction for the delivery of certain policies, justifying the need for institutions to be operating on a regional stage. Above the local and below the national level, to optimise the opportunities offered by backwash and spread effects and to address both the need for economies of scale and a bottom up approach, the region should be involved in the allocation and growth functions of government in the economy.

Promoting endogenous development through an appropriate mix of inward investment, indigenous enterprise support, skills and training organised and co-ordinated at the regional level, has been applied as some of the justification for decentralisation of economic development powers in the UK (Newlands, 1997; Tomaney and Mawson, 2002) and in other countries (e.g., Moreno, 2002, on Spain; Cappellin, 1997, on Italy, France, etc). Nevertheless, most of this evidence comes from large countries where regions are themselves of some size and often based on ad hoc administrative boundaries alone. We are less well informed by the literature about how regions within smaller countries should be considered when determining the most appropriate jurisdiction for economic allocation and growth functions, though Newlands (1999) and Danson, Hill and Lloyd (1997) discuss these issues and note the paucity of evidence.

As reported in the Introduction, in pursuing economic development many small nations, whether independent or within a larger territory, have adopted the regional development agency (RDA) approach favoured by Ireland and Scotland. Regions of all sizes progressively have followed this model of intervention, seeking to capture the benefits of having an RDA to deliver key economic strategies and policies (Halkier and Danson, 1997; Halkier, Danson and Damborg, 1998; Danson, Halkier, and Cameron, 2000).

THE REGIONAL DEVELOPMENT AGENCY

Regional development agencies (RDAs) are semi-autonomous institutions which have played an important part in the process of balancing the benefits of tailored "bottom-up" initiatives with the economies of scale and scope offered by national "top-down" policies. An RDA can be defined as "a regionally based, publicly financed institution outside the mainstream of central and local government administration designed to promote economic development" (Halkier and Danson, 1997). In their studies of such bodies across the European continent, a model RDA is defined by Halkier and Danson (1997: 245) as a body which, first, organisationally is in a semi-autonomous position vis-à-vis its sponsoring political authority; second, supports mainly indigenous firms by means of "soft" policy instruments; and, third, is a multifunctional and integrated agency, the level of which may be determined by the range of policy instruments it uses.

Following a Europe-wide study of organisations and agencies, they derive a typology of RDAs, defining "model", "potential" and non-RDAs:

Table 3.1: Model RDAs

Typology	Description
Model RDAs	Relatively large organisations with mixed-traditional policy profiles
Potential RDAs	Medium to small organisations with mixed-new profiles
Non RDAs	Relatively small organisations specialising in new policy areas

Source: Halkier and Danson (1997: p. 245).

More recent evidence may suggest that this typology is breaking down, apart from in the UK where the recently introduced English RDAs have been modelled on the initial Scottish Development Agency model, and Scottish Enterprise has continued to attract additional responsibilities and roles (Brown and Danson, 2003). This inconsistent pattern of evolution of the development agency implies that the best practice model of even a few years ago may no longer be appropriate in 2003. To the extent that smaller but autonomous RDAs are being fostered and created, not least from the older larger agencies, there is the opportunity to insert institutions in novel levels in the overall framework.

In the UK context, RDAs have been seen as a method of reducing the level of localised market failure in accordance with and in support of the government's macroeconomic regional policy instruments and objectives. Fairley and Lloyd (1998) have explored the principle of market failure as it applies to development agencies, and their perceptions are consistent with recent developments as reviewed above, with the Scottish agencies for example tending to widen the definition to allow a broader degree of policy intervention than first envisaged. Fairley and Lloyd also incorporated the concept of "government failure" into their discussions as a reason for restricting intervention; to an extent this would support devolving powers to a quasi non-governmental body more oriented to the needs of the market.

The economic argument in support of development agencies — as the most effective tool for addressing such local market failures as risk aversion in the financial sector, poor market information, externalities in the provision of infrastructure and training, and problems associated with rapid growth and technological change (Danson, Lloyd and Newlands, 1993) — rests on several advantages over other methods of policy implementation which have been considered, such as local authorities, central government departments, and private sector-led bodies such as the English UDCs (Urban Development Corporations).

Able to intervene and interact with the economy at the most appropriate jurisdictional level (Armstrong, 1997), regional agencies can bring substantial resources to bear on problems of local economic development, combining regional, industrial and training policies and resources on specific projects, for instance. They represent the manageable "bottom-up" alternative, avoiding the bewildering maze of local initiatives now present in many areas, but also flexible and receptive to the specific needs of the indigenous industry within the region. A number of responsibilities which otherwise may be split between different departments or quasi-government agencies — such as the provision of property and sites, the attraction of inward investment, brownfield regeneration, cluster strategies, and urban redevelopment — by being located within a single organisation can reduce costs and realise synergies (Moore and Booth, 1986).

Operationally, RDAs frequently combine area and sectoral strategies nowadays often as cluster strategies, and offer comprehensive business services, both functions that could be more difficult to deliver if these were spread across departments and agencies. More crucial perhaps, as they are at arms' length from government, RDAs can develop a degree of operational freedom and credibility which regional departments of government or departments of regional government may lack. They may be able, therefore, to have potential leverage over significant private funds, representing a strong advantage over a national parliament or regional assembly. In times of high mobility of multinational capital, such compromises may be necessary to attract and retain jobs, incomes and technologies. Their position outside the mainstream government apparatus may allow public policies to be pursued without invoking the ghosts of interventionism or state dirigisme. This can make the development agency approach to regional economic development more acceptable to the full range of social partners, without necessarily undermining accountability.

Besides these short-term policy interventions focusing on the particular needs of enterprises and workforces of the area, RDAs can also adopt a long-term perspective. A strategic view can allow policies to be followed which are to the long run benefit of the region, but which may be unpopular in the immediate period. Thus, relatively isolated from short term political intervention and manoeuvrings, there should be the potential to restructure the economy in a planned way that would lift the development path of indigenous industry onto a higher level, achieving greater endogenous growth. It can be argued that distance from central government could well be fundamental to the success of such a strategy. Although the operating environment may be more closely attuned to the needs of local enterprise, a regional development agency can also instil a sense of local ownership of economic development strategies while demonstrating a political commitment to the long-term growth of the economy as a whole. The potential to promote and encourage trust and cooperation through such an institutional approach can engender further virtuous circles of growth and development in ways that a regional parliament and local authorities could not.

REGIONS AND RDAS WITHIN SMALLER NATIONS

A significant problem in the introduction of the RDAs into the English regions (DETR, 1998) has been the failure to recognise the difficulties caused by the continued existence of the plethora of bodies and programmes in each region; in the Scottish cases, such additions to the institutional infrastructure were introduced after the Highlands and Islands Development Board and the Scottish Development Agency were established. In the words of the UK Trade and Industry Committee, LECs (the network of local enterprise companies in Scotland) are "able to deliver national schemes and programmes flexibly, in response to local needs and circumstances" (Trade and Industry Committee, 1995).

The importance of political scale and of being able to intervene to address problems over the delivery of services in a territory have been approached in number of ways. With the introduction of the European Partnership programming model for regions, there have been opportunities to consider the dissemination of good practice across the region, and for problems of overlap, duplication and gaps in provision to be acknowledged.

So, despite the recognised advantages held by RDAs as discussed above, and the well-tested modes of RDAs delivering policies and programmes, increasingly they have been operating in partnership with other agencies and organisations. It has been suggested (Cameron and Danson, 2000) that while such means of intervention are well established and apparently accepted (Danson, Fairley, Lloyd and Turok, 1999), there are potential negative implications also. Having created the RDA as an institution effectively at arms-length from government, some of the advantages of this autonomy may be lost through the compromises and shared agenda necessary in successful partnerships (Cameron and Danson, 2000). While there are undoubted advantages to the closeness and cohesion of small regions and nations, there is still a need to counter any failure to achieve economies of scale offered in large federal economies with their capacities to transfer resources between regions (Kellermann and Schmidt, 1997; Haynes et al, 1997).

Recently, it has been proposed that there is a new wave of evolution in the history of the RDA underway (as discussed at Scottish Enterprise/EURADA seminar, Brussels, October 2002), with smaller dedicated agencies being established or transferred out from the RDA itself. The disengagement of parts of Scottish Enterprise and Highlands and Islands Enterprise in Scotland to merge with other elements of the public and QUANGO sector as two new non-departmental bodies (NDPBs): "Careers Scotland" and "Communities Scotland", are two examples of this sort of transformation. To date there is nothing to suggest, however, that these agencies will not continue to operate as their parent bodies, and so as traditional development agencies within the accepted typologies outlined earlier (Halkier and Danson, 1997). In particular, in a continuation of past practices they are having to work in partnership with other organisations and with the RDAs especially. Their degrees of autonomy are under question, therefore, with the responsibility and powers over their operations effectively shared with the government department and the RDAs themselves.

This exercise to balance the need for democratic accountability with the advantages of RDAs, and of having the capacity to be semi-autonomous, is likely to be repeated across the continent as the drivers for change and adaptation impact ever more strongly in the coming years. With more "case law" and

experience available, it should be possible to address such issues better informed than at present. Since its re-establishment,
the Parliament in Edinburgh, Scotland, in particular, has been
reviewing its configuration of institutions, and so reconsidering
whether matters of institutional thickness and capacity are
paramount as previously suggested (Macleod, 1997). Concerns
over institutional overlap and duplication have been seen as
more damaging than gaps in provision with regard to the delivery of local economic development services (ELLC, 2000).

Similarly, the moves to introduce new institutions — local
economic fora — at a regional level within Scotland point to a
desire to recognise that the advantages of the partnership
model are applicable for a jurisdiction above the locality itself.
These areas have tended to be at the level of the local enterprise company (the constituent parts of the Scottish Enterprise
network) and so include one or more local government authorities within their boundaries (Danson et al., 2000). With the EU
structural fund areas being laid over these also, there are questions over the definition of the region itself.

Whether administrative, travel to work, or some other functional area is adopted as the "region", the definition is important but problematic. In some instances, these will produce
congruent boundaries; in others the respective spaces may be
changing over time, as for example commuting patterns
change, or conflicting between level and purpose. Data problems can exacerbate these difficulties and inconsistencies. The
adoption of political jurisdictions themselves may depend on
tax and spending powers and responsibilities, which are not
well aligned with the functions of the region. In Germany and
the US there is a uniform configuration of such matters across
the country, in Spain and the UK devolution has been introduced asymmetrically producing no unique pattern of regions.

However, the endogenous growth theories, which are taken
as the reference points for many strategic interventions and
policies provide some implicit guidance to resolve this. Communities and so societies which adopt such a regime should be
taking cognisance of the significance of such notions and concepts as "cohesion, trust and cooperation, consensus, untraded
interdependencies", all of which seem to be more likely to be

identified within areas accepted as "coherent regions" with some inherent homogeneity (Graham and Hart, 1999). For small countries and stateless nations, the national level may be sufficient to provide this cohesion while the regional may be administratively defined. Perhaps supporting this approach, Florida (2000) has argued that "Quality-of-place is the missing piece of the puzzle. To compete successfully in the age of talent, regions must make quality-of-place a central element of their economic development efforts." The importance of such "social capital" in providing the most conducive environment for inclusive and dynamic growth has been progressively promoted in the literature for the last decade (Putnam, 1992). A coherent, self-confident and prosperous region is promised in the scenario, which seeks to embrace the benefits offered by the new economic geography.

From the research on the necessities for successful regional economic development, a number of factors seem to be appearing. These range from those traditionally supported as physical infrastructure, airports and other transport links, to the softer investments offered by higher education institutions especially but by human capital formation more generally. Discussions on the invisible factors of local economic development (Doeringer et al., 1987) have embraced entrepreneurship and enterprise, networking and partnership, and other cultural elements which regional science is perhaps less capable of evaluating in terms of their effects. Some of these have been introduced above, but undoubtedly they are individually and collectively increasingly seen as critical components in the growth and development of the region and nation.

That they are primarily defined as supply side interventions in the economy, compared with the Keynesian approach of the post-war period, is also notable. In open, WTO and EU-regulated economies, nations and regions are considered to compete through such factors (Porter, 1990) rather than through their natural endowments, geographical location or industrial heritage.

CONCLUSIONS AND FUTURES

This chapter has argued that to address differential rates of economic prosperity, there is a strong rationale for regional institutions being involved in regional economic development through the application of allocation and growth strategies. Because of changes in the global environment and restrictions on traditional industrial and regional policy regimes, endogenous drivers for regeneration have become more favoured in recent times. Consequently, many regions across the world have introduced regional development agencies as the preferred means to exercise their functions and powers, to deliver the strategies and policies appropriate to their economies and communities. However, despite the ubiquitous presence of such institutions, context is critical to their degrees of success.

First, the definition of the region itself is not insignificant given the importance ascribed to certain notions — of cohesion, networking and interdependencies — in the theories underpinning endogenous growth. Clusters and other forms of intervention in the local economic landscape depend on synergies between key players, while most regional economic development strategies are delivered through partnerships and rely upon successful partnership working. The very nature of such approaches to delivering strategy, involving compromise, conflict resolution and shared agenda and resources, however, may undermine the rationale for RDAs as bodies at arms' length from government.

Faced with a hostile global environment, it may not be appropriate for the region in the small nation, therefore, to separate the formation and the delivery of its regional economic development strategies. As the key role of the RDA may have to be constrained anyway to ensure democratic accountability in an inclusive society, the further restriction of its powers through participation in European and other local partnerships may render the difference between semi-autonomous agency and regional government department marginal.

Compounding this lack of definitive prescription, many of the theories and experiences are based on the structures and conditions in large federal countries, with Germany and the US in particular featuring in this literature. Further, this research material has tended to neglect rural, peripheral and island environments. To a greater extent than in the recent past, this suggests that there is a need to learn from similar areas, whereas in the times of dependence on pursuing mobile foreign capital and inward investment competition between the countries of the Celtic periphery precluded such co-operation.

It cannot be denied that there have been different performances between the Celtic nations over the last 15 years. The ability of an independent state within the EU to grow and to develop its economy can be contrasted with the constraints on Scotland, Wales and Northern Ireland. From having the benefits of being insignificant (Mackay, 2003), they, and Scotland in particular, are now suffering from being in the limelight offered by devolution. Without a considered needs assessment and constitutional framework, this devolution "settlement" may represent a poisoned chalice, with the advantages of Irish freedom of action ultimately more attractive.

In this context, for the first time in a millennium, common cause and partnership across these nations and between their regions may be more appropriate than indifference or rivalry. They are operating in an environment, which disadvantages them to the same extent, with enlargement and deepening of the EU exacerbating their shared peripherality. From delivering a model approach to competing for the investment of multinational capital, the regional development agency, perhaps Ireland and Scotland now can and must extend the potential of partnership into new dimensions of economic development, not least in research, evaluation and lobbying?

References

Anyadike-Danes, M., Fothergill, S., Glyn, A., Grieve Smith, J., Kitson, M., Martin, R., Rowthorn, R., Turok, I., Tyler, P. and Webster, D. (2001), *Labour's New Regional Policy: An Assessment*, Regional Studies Association, Seaford.

Armstrong, H. (1997), "Regional-level jurisdictions and economic regeneration initiatives" in Danson, M., Lloyd, G. and Hill, S. (eds.) "Regional Government and Economic Development", *European Research in Regional Science* Vol. 7. London: Pion, pp. 26-46.

Bachtler, J. (2002), "Reflections on reform of the Structural Funds" paper to *RSA Evaluation and Regional Policy Conference*, Aix en Provence, 2 June.

Bachtler, J., Josserand, F. and Michie, R. (2002), *EU Enlargement and the Reform of the Structural Funds: The Implications for Scotland*, scotecon, University of Stirling.

Benneworth, P., Danson, M., Raines, P. and Whittam, G. (2003), "Confusing clusters? Making sense of the cluster approach in theory and practice", *European Planning Studies*, Vol. 11, No. 5, July (Forthcoming).

Brand, S., Hill, S. and Munday, M. (2000), "Assessing the impacts of foreign manufacturing on regional economies: the cases of Wales, Scotland and the West Midlands" *Regional Studies*. Vol. 34, 345-355.

Brown, R. and Danson, M. (2003), "Regional Development Agencies: which model for a small country?", paper to Fourth Israeli/British & Irish Regional Science Workshop, 19-20 May, Edinburgh.

Cappellin, R. (1997), "Federalism and the network paradigm: guidelines for a new approach in national regional policy." In Danson, M., Lloyd, G. and Hill, S. (eds.) "Regional Government and Economic Development", *European Research in Regional Science* Vol. 7. London: Pion, pp. 47-67.

Cameron, G. and Danson, M. (1999), "The European partnership model and the changing role of regional development agencies. A regional development and organisation perspective." In M. Danson, H Halkier and G. Cameron *Governance, Institutional Change and Development*. London: Ashgate, pp. 11-36.

CEC (Commission of the European Communities) (2003), *European Employment Strategy*, http://europa.eu.int/comm/employment_social/employment_strategy/index_en.htm

Charles, D. (2003), "The emergence of a multi-scalar science policy?", *ESRC/RSA Regions and Science Policy Conference*, 8-9 May, London.

Danson, M., Deakins, D., Whittam, G., and Fairley, J. (2000), "Inquiry into Local Economic Development: A Map of Economic Development Support Across Scotland", Annexe E, Volume 2, *Inquiry into the Delivery of Local Economic Development Services in Scotland*, SP Paper 109, Enterprise and Lifelong Learning Committee, Scottish Parliament, Edinburgh.

Danson, M., Fairley, J., Lloyd, G. and Turok, I. (1997), *The Governance of European Structural Funds: The Experience of the Scottish Regional Partnerships*. Paper 10. Brussels: Scotland Europa.

Danson, M., Halkier, H. and Cameron, G. (2000), *Governance, Institutional Change and Regional Development*, London: Ashgate.

Danson, M., Helinska-Hughes, E. and Hughes, M. (2002), "The Central and Eastern European challenge for FDI: Lessons from the Celtic periphery", *Journal of East-West Business,* Vol. 8, No. 2, 85-104.

Danson, M., Hill, S. and Lloyd, G. (1997), Introduction in "Regional Government and Economic Development", *European Research in Regional Science* Vol. 7. London: Pion.

Danson, M., G. Lloyd and D. Newlands (1993), "The role of regional development agencies", in Harrison, R. and Hart, M. (eds.) *Spatial Policy in a Divided Nation*, London: Jessica Kingsley Publishers.

DETR (1998), *Regional Development Agencies Act 1998*, London, HMSO.

Doeringer. P. et al. (1987), *Invisible Factors in Local Economic Development*. New York: OUP.

Dunford, M. (2003), "Theorising regional economic performance and the changing territorial division of labour", *Regional Studies* Vol. 37, forthcoming.

Enterprise and Lifelong Learning Committee (ELLC) (2000), *Inquiry into the Delivery of Local Economic Development Services in Scotland*, SP Paper 109, Scottish Parliament, Edinburgh.

Fairley, J. and Lloyd, G. (1998), "Enterprise in Scotland — A mid-term assessment of an institutional innovation for economic development." *Regional Development Agencies in Europe*. London: Jessica Kingsley Publishers.

Fielding, A (1991), "Migration and social mobility: South East England as an escalator region", *Regional Studies*, Vol. 26, No. 1, 1-15.

Florida, R. (2000), *The Rise of the Creative Class and How It's Transforming Work, Leisure, Community and Everyday Life,* New York: Basic Books.

Graham, B. and Hart, M. (1999), "Cohesion and diversity in the European Union: irreconcilable forces?", *Regional Studies,* Vol. 33, 259-268.

Green, A. (2001), "The Scottish Labour Market – Future Scenarios", Issue Paper No. 3, Futureskills Scotland, Glasgow.

Halkier, H., Danson, M., and Damborg, C. (eds) (1998), "Regional development agencies in Europe: An introduction and framework for analysis." *Regional Development Agencies in Europe*. London: Jessica Kingsley Publishers.

Halkier, H. and Danson, M. (1997), "Regional Development Agencies in Western Europe: A Survey of Characteristics and Trends". *European Urban and Regional Studies,* Vol. 4, No. 3, 243-256.

Haynes, K., Maas, G., Stough, R. and Riggle, J. (1997), "Regional governance and economic development: Lessons from federal states." In Danson, M., Hill, S. and Lloyd, G. (eds.). *Regional Governance and Economic Development.* European Research in Regional Science 7, London: Pion, pp. 68-84.

Howells, J (2003), "Science and Technology Policy, Innovation and Regional Economic Development", *ESRC/RSA Regions and Science Policy Conference*, 8-9 May, London.

Jensen, C. and Leijon, S. (2000), "Persuasive storytelling about the reform process: The case of the West Sweden region", in Danson, M., Halkier, H. and Cameron, G. (eds) *Governance, Institutional Change and Regional Development*, London: Ashgate, pp. 172-194.

Jeffery, C. and Mawson, J. (2002), "Introduction: Beyond the White Paper on the English Regions", *Regional Studies,* Vol. 36, No. 7, 715-720.

Kellermann, K. and Schmidt, H. (1997), "Regional growth and convergence in a tax-sharing system" In Danson, M., Hill, S. and Lloyd, G. (eds.). *Regional Governance and Economic Development.* European Research in Regional Science 7, London: Pion, pp. 210-228.

King, D. (1984), *Fiscal Tiers: The Economics of Multi Level Government*, London: George Allen and Unwin.

Krugman P. (1997), "Good News from Ireland: A Geographical Perspective", in A. Gray (ed.), *International Perspectives on the Irish Economy*, Dublin: Indecon Economic Consultants, pp. 38-53.

Mackay, R. (2003), "Twenty-five years of regional development", *Regional Studies*, Vol. 37, No. 3, 303-317.

MacLeod, G. (1997), "'Institutional thickness' and industrial governance in Lowland Scotland" *Area,* Vol. 29, 299-311.

Martin, R. and Townroe, P. eds. (1992), *Regional Development in the British Isles in the Nineteen Nineties*, London: Jessica Kingsley.

McCann, P. and Sheppard, S. (2003), "Human capital, higher education and graduate migration: An analysis of Scottish and Welsh students", paper to RSAI British and Irish Section conference, Brighton.

Moore, C. and Booth, S. (1986), "From comprehensive regeneration to privatization: the search for effective area strategies." In W. Lever and C. Moore (eds) *The City in Transition*, Oxford: Clarendon Press, pp. 107-119.

Moreno, L. (2002), "Decentralization in Spain", *Regional Studies*, 36, 4, 399-408.

Musgrave, R. (1959), *The Theory of Public Finance*, New York: McGraw Hill.

Myrdal, G. (1958), *Economic Theory and Underdeveloped Regions*, London: Methuen

National Development Plan: 2000-2006 (2000), Dublin: Stationery Office

National Development Strategy: 2002-2020: People, Places and Potential (2002), Dublin: Stationery Office

Newlands, D. (1999), "The economic powers and potential of a devolved Scottish Parliament: Lessons from economic theory and European experience", in Newlands, D. and McCarthy, J. (eds) *Governing Scotland: Problems and Prospects. The Economic Impact of the Scottish Parliament*. London: Ashgate, pp. 11-24.

Newlands, D. (1997), "The economic powers and potential of a devolved Scottish parliament: lessons from economic theory and European experience" In Danson, M., Hill, S. and Lloyd, G. (eds.). *Regional Governance and Economic Development*. European Research in Regional Science 7, London: Pion, pp. 109-127.

O'Leary, E. (2001), "Convergence of living standards among Irish regions: The role of productivity, profit outflows and demography, 1960-1996", *Regional Studies*, 35, (3) 197-205.

Phelps, N. and Raines, P. (eds.) (2003), *The New Competition for Inward Investment: Companies, Institutions and Territorial Development*, London: Edward Elgar.

Porter, M. (1990), *The Competitive Advantage of Nations*, London: Macmillan.

Parr, J., Hewings, G., Sohn, J. and Nazara, S. (2002), "Agglomeration and trade: Some additional perspectives", *Regional Studies*, 36, 6, 675-684.

Putnam, R. D. (1992), *Making Democracy Work: Civic Traditions in Modern Italy*, Princeton: Princeton University Press.

Scottish Executive (2001), *A Smart Successful Scotland*, Edinburgh.

Scottish Executive (2000), *Framework for Economic Development*, Edinburgh.

Smith, D. (1989), *North and South: Britain's Economic, Social and Political Divide*. London: Penguin.

Taylor, J. and Wren, C. (1997), "UK regional policy: An evaluation", *Regional Studies*, Vol. 31, 835-848.

Chapter 4

INDUSTRY PERFORMANCE AND REGIONAL GROWTH: LESSONS FOR IRISH POLICYMAKERS

John Dewhurst

INTRODUCTION

The recent development of a direct regional initiative in Ireland in some ways, at least, mirrors the experience in Great Britain, where regional policy appears to be becoming increasingly devolved, in particular through the devolution of powers to the Welsh Assembly and the Scottish Executive and the establishment of the English Regional Development Agencies. Although, particularly in England, this policy is at an early stage the indications are that it has led to an increasing local interest in regional development and in the possibilities of making local initiatives to foster that development. To the extent that these initiatives can be tailored to local needs and circumstances the replacement of a top-down approach by a more bottom-up approach might be thought an improvement.

At the same time there may be some adverse welfare effects of such a policy. One of the priorities of the Scottish Executive appears to be the attraction to Scotland of foreign direct investment. In an age of globalisation this presents clear challenges but also is likely, if successful, to bring rewards. But it is abundantly clear that this is not a peculiarly Scottish desire. Indeed the search for foreign investment seems to be a common feature of most if not all areas in the UK if not Europe. Ireland is often taken as a shining example of the success that such a policy can bring. To attract inward investment a region must sell itself to an inward investor. This in itself is a costly exercise. However, as many regions are searching for such investment, the region is operating in a competitive market in which it has a differentiated product to sell. As the costs involved in persuading companies to locate in the region can be viewed as advertising costs they can be expected to be rather higher than would be the case if the region were not in competition with others. However it is clear from casual empiricism, if from nowhere else, that these "advertising" costs are not the only costs that region needs to outlay to attract inward investment. To win such investment in the face of competition from other regions may well require large prior investment in capital infrastructure such as transport networks, suitable factory facilities and environmental enhancement. Although much of this investment may be recouped on the establishment of in-migrant firm to the particular area it is clear that any firm specific investment of this type that is made may be lost if that particular firm decides not to locate in the region.

As a result there is likely to be excessive duplication of efforts to attract incoming firms and a resultant misuse of national and indeed European resources. At the national level in the UK this is controlled to a limited extent by attempts to ensure that different regions do not bid against each other for the same inward investment. Whether the Irish government would allow, through the IDA, different regions to bid for the same project is, perhaps, unlikely. Early indications suggest that this would not be the case. There appears to be much less control exercised at a European level. In this particular form of regional policy therefore there may be a case for a greater degree of control from Brussels than currently exists.

Foreign Direct Investment is not the only sphere in which competition between regions exists. Another area is the area of promotion of high-tech/bio-tech industries. In the UK there are clusters of bio-tech firms centred on Cambridge and to a lesser extent Glasgow in Scotland. It is clear that other regions see the success of these developments as possible models for successful regional development. Both Dundee and York, for example, are marketing themselves as bio-tech cities. In the Irish case it also seems that the development agencies are to promote the new gateways as centres for high value-added clusters (National Spatial Strategy, 2002). It is reasonable to suppose that the market is finite in that there is a limit to the number of firms that can be set up in this area at least over a medium term planning horizon. It is also reasonable to assume that regions are not equally endowed with the attributes that encourage the setting up of such firms. It is clear assuming that they had the discretion to decide that some regions may perceive that their endowments are unlikely to prove attractive and not pursue such a development strategy.

However, those cities and regions that do compete for development in the same sector could be likened to firms pursuing technology improvements. Here the industrial economics literature on research and development may prove a fruitful starting point for analysis. The situation is similar to a non-tournament model of research and development with endogenous rewards in that there can be several winners and the extent of the gains will be dependent, to some extent at least, on the efforts regions make in fostering the development (Dasgupta and Stiglitz, 1980). If the parallel is valid, then three interesting results arise from some versions of this type of model. First, there will be too many regions chasing the development. Second, each region will do too little to foster such development. Third, the collection of regions will expend too many resources on the development. Again there would appear to be a case for some national or community wide control of such expenditures if we wish to maximise the gains to society. Given that every region, to a greater or lesser extent, will be trying to foster its own development such control may not be immediately politically attractive.

Often, it appears foreign direct investment and the development of high-tech, bio-tech or more generally high value added clusters are interrelated. Although spin-offs and indigenous start-ups, especially perhaps from the university sector, are seen as important in the dynamic of a successful cluster it is also apparent that entrance into the cluster by firms from elsewhere can be an important stimulus.

Although not doubting the part played by such clusters in the fortunes of some regions, the justification of policies of stimulating development in such a manner at a regional level might be argued to be based more on example rather than on general principles. Often the argument seems to be that because we see a successful cluster operating in region X then such a cluster or a similar one will be successful in region Y. The extent to which initiatives to stimulate development in this manner can overcome any resource, structural or location disadvantages the region may have is a complex question that, perhaps, receives less attention than it might.

It is pertinent to point out that although such attempts to foster regional economic growth have short-term effects, they are essentially medium to long-term initiatives. So long as there is not 100 per cent displacement, the attraction of a foreign investor will immediately increase employment in the region. However the continued existence of the new firm might lead to technology spillovers to other firms in the same industry and to providers of inputs to the new firm. Successful new firms may in addition prove to be a magnet for further growth in the industry, either through attracting further inward investment or through diversification of the original firm.

In the quantitative section of the chapter that follows an attempt is made to examine, in an exploratory manner using data for Great Britain, whether there is any discernable link first between regional growth and the region's industrial specialisation in an industry or the growth of industries in the region and second whether those industries whose fortunes seem to be related to that of the region in which they are well established or in which they prosper have a distinctive nature linked to measures that may be derived from input-output accounts. If there were not to be such a typography of industries that discriminated industries well according to how they are associated with the region's fortunes, this would lend support to the idea that regional policies designed to stimulate a particular region cannot reliably be borrowed from successful regions elsewhere. This result would have clear implications for Irish regional policy.

AN EMPIRICAL EXPLORATION

This section reports a number of preliminary, exploratory findings on the association between elements of industrial structure and regional growth in the medium term in Great Britain. As with all exercises of this kind, results can be affected by the levels of spatial and industrial disaggregation utilised. In this chapter results for three levels of regional disaggregation are reported, for NUTS 3, NUTS 2 and NUTS 1 regions of Great Britain. Figures for GDP for NUTS regions in Great Britain are available from 1994 but to permit correspondence between the GDP figures and the industrial structure data the starting date for the exercise reported here is 1995 (UK National Statistics, 2002a). The variables relating to industrial structure are derived from Census of Employment data. As there was no Census in 1994 and the most recent Census was taken in 1998, the three-year period 1995-1998 is the period examined (UK National Statistics, 2002b). Employment data from the Census is available at various levels of industrial disaggregation down to the four-digit level. In this exercise the 123 industries separately identified in the 1995 Input-Output tables for the UK are chosen as this allows a classification of industrial sectors according to measures that can be derived from that input-output table (UK National Statistics, 2002c). It should be noted that the figures reported by the Census of Employment exclude, for most regional disaggregations, data on agriculture. Accordingly the figures reported below are based on non-agricultural employment only.

The first question the chapter seeks to answer is whether regions with relative specialisation in any particular industries grew significantly faster than regions that lacked that specialisation. For each industry in turn one may calculate the correlation coefficient between the regional growth rates and the initial (1995) shares of employment of the industry. The positive significant (at a two-sided 5 per cent level) results are shown in Table 4.1. There are a number of features of the table that are worthy of comment. First, if the series were completely random then, given the size of the test, one might expect three industries to occur in each column. Thus it would appear that there is informational content in the results. Second, for 11 of the 23 industries listed the correlation is significant at whatever level of regional disaggregation one considers. Third, the majority of industries listed (17/23) are service sector industries, predominately business service activities.

Table 4.1: Industry Shares and Regional Growth (Positive Association)

NUTS Level 3	NUTS Level 2	NUTS Level 1
Grain mill prods, starch		
Publishing, printing, reproduction of recording material	Publishing, printing, reproduction of recording material	Publishing, printing, Reproduction of recording material
	Pesticides & other agro-chemical products	Pesticides & other agro-chemical products
	Office machinery, computers	
TV radio transmitters, line		
	Medical, precision, optical instruments	
Wholesale trade	Wholesale trade	Wholesale trade
		Air transport
		Supporting activities for transport
Post & counter activities	Post & counter activities	Post & counter activities
Telecommunications	Telecommunications	Telecommunications
Financial intermediation		
Insurance pensions funds		
Activities ancillary to financial intermediation	Activities ancillary to financial intermediation	
Own property real estate activities		
Real estate activities	Real estate activities	Real estate activities
Computer and related activities	Computer and related activities	Computer and related activities
R&D	R&D	R&D
Accountancy	Accountancy	
Market research, business services	Market research, business services	Market research, business services
Advertising	Advertising	Advertising
Other business services	Other business services	Other business services
Other service activities	Other service activities	Other service activities

Source: UK National Statistics (2002a; 2002b)

The industries with significant negative associations with growth rates are shown in Table 4.2. Here there is rather more variation across regional disaggregations, relatively greater representation of the primary and manufacturing sectors and no business service industry.

Table 4.2: Industry Shares and Regional Growth (Negative Association)

NUTS Level 3	NUTS Level 2	NUTS Level 1
Forestry, logging and related service activities	Forestry, logging and related service activities	
Fishing		
		Mining coal, lignite, peat
Extraction of crude petroleum & natural gas		
Fish, fish products, fruit and veg	Fish, fish products, fruit and veg	
	Bread, biscuits, pastry cakes	Bread, biscuits, pastry cakes
Alcoholic beverages	Alcoholic beverages	
Wood and wood products	Wood and wood products	Wood and wood products
	Pulp, paper, paperboard	
	Coke, refined petrol prods, nuclear fuel	
Other inorganic basic chemicals		
	Structural metal products	Structural metal products
Building, repairing ships	Building, repairing ships	
Construction	Construction	Construction
	Other land transport	
Human health and vets		Human health and vets
Social work		Social work

Source: UK National Statistics (2002a; 2002b)

The UK input-output tables can be used to measure (admittedly at a national level) various facets of industries, in particular (a) the extent to which the industry's product is sold to households rather than other industries, (b) the extent of the backward linkage exhibited by the industry and (c) the ratio of value added in the gross output in the industry. However there is no evidence that the industries in Table 4.1 differ significantly from those in Table 4.2 in any of these three respects. In particular it is worth noting that the fact that a region had a degree of specialisation in an industry with strong backward linkages at the start of the period, or in one with relatively high value added, gives little indication of the region's growth rate over the period considered.

By implication this suggests that policies designed to support and encourage such industries are not, necessarily, certain to improve the relative growth prospects of the region in question. Such industries are sometimes described as having "cluster potential". The suggestion here is that a blanket concentration on support for such industries, without a more detailed analysis of their place and role in the regional economy, may be misplaced. In the case of Ireland it may be that even if regions have industrial structures that appear to offer scope for cluster economies they may not grow significantly faster than regions elsewhere.

It is also of interest to examine the associations between the rate of employment growth in individual industries and the regional growth rates over the period. Those industries whose growth rates exhibited significant positive correlation with the regional growth rates are shown in Table 4.3 and those with significant negative growth rates in Table 4.4. Perhaps the first thing to note is that there are not more industries in Table 4.3.

Table 4.3: Industry Growth and Regional Growth (Positive Association)

NUTS Level 3	NUTS Level 2	NUTS Level 1
Forestry, logging and related service activities		Forestry, logging and related service activities
Prepared animal feeds		
Other textiles		
Basic iron and steel		
		Agriculture and forestry equipment
	Building, repairing ships	
	Gas	Gas
Construction	Construction	
Air transport	Air transport	
	Real estate activities	Real estate activities
Computer and related activities	Computer and related activities	Computer and related activities
	Advertising	
Other business services	Other business services	
Education		
		Sewage and refuse activities

Source: UK National Statistics (2002a; 2002b)

Table 4.4: Industry Growth and Regional Growth (Negative Association)

NUTS Level 3	NUTS Level 2	NUTS Level 1
Pulp, paper, paperboard		
		Pharmaceuticals etc.
	Soap, detergents, perfumes, toiletries	
Other chemical products		
		Rubber products
	Structural metal products	Structural metal products
Office machinery, computers	Office machinery, computers	Office machinery, computers
Retail trade	Retail trade	Retail trade
		Water transport
Telecommunications	Telecommunications	
	Public admin and defence	Public admin and defence
	Human health an vets	
	Other service activities	Other service activities

Source: UK National Statistics (2002a; 2002b)

Clearly a relatively high growth rate in a region does not necessarily imply that all or even a majority of the industries in the
region are performing significantly better than elsewhere. At
the same time there is no obvious reason why the industries
listed in Table 4.4 should behave in a counter-cyclical manner.
There is also no obvious correspondence between industries in
Tables 4.3 and 4.4 with the division between industries given in
Tables 4.1 and 4.2. Once again comparing the industries in Table 4.3 with those in Table 4.4 in terms of the variables derived
from the input-output tables indicates no significant differences
in any of the three cases. It is suggested here that relatively
high levels of regional growth does not affect all industries in
the same beneficial way, that there are a non-negligible set of
industries that, in the UK at least, appear to grow faster in regions where overall growth is less marked and that industries
that have grown relatively quickly are not necessarily those that
have "cluster potential". It may be that in highly open regional
economies inter-regional and international factors in particular
perhaps competitiveness may be more important in explaining
an industry's regional performance rather than intra-regional
relationships.

As a final remark casual observation would suggest that
many regions would like to foster the development of high-
valued added industries with strong backward linkages into the
regional economy. Using national data for the 123 industries
considered in this chapter, Figure 4.1 shows that this may not
be an easy task. In some senses, of course, this is as one would
expect. The Gross Output of any industry is the sum of Value
Added and Intermediate Inputs. The backward linkage of any
industry is dependent, to some extent at least, on the volume of
its domestic intermediate inputs. Any increase in such backward linkages, whilst keeping value added constant, would
only arise if more intermediate inputs were domestically
sourced rather than imported. An industrially disaggregated
analysis of a time series of input-output tables might be necessary to analyse this further.

Figure 4.1: Value Added to Gross Output and Backward Linkage

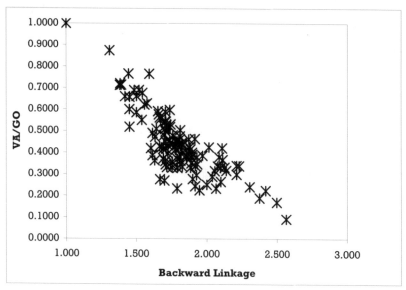

Source: UK National Statistics (2002a; 2002c).

CONCLUSION

The results reported in the previous section may appear to be confusing and not to convey any positive policy insights or guidelines. However, that, in itself, may be the important lesson to be learnt. There is no doubt that regional growth is determined through a myriad of complex causal channels, some of which may be influenced by policy. It seems more than plausible that sympathetic regional initiatives may strengthen the economy of the region in the short, medium and long terms. What the results indicate, however, is that it is very difficult to "pick winners" when choosing industrial sectors to support and encourage by reference to what is happening elsewhere. In the industrial support arena it would appear from this admittedly exploratory exercise that regions are better focusing on policies tailored to their own particular circumstances than adopting a more generalist simplistic strategy. This suggests that a national blueprint for regional policy might not be expected to perform well across all regions of a country and that regional inputs to the regional policy process might be essential. Although this might appear to be true for the UK, with 11 regions, the implications might not be as strong when one considers the Irish NUTS 2 regions, of which there are only two. However, for Ireland's eight NUTS 3 planning regions, the conclusion might be just as valid.

References

Dasgupta, P. and Stiglitz, J. (1980), "Industrial Structure and the Nature of Innovative Activity", *Economic Journal,* Vol. 90, 260-293.

National Spatial Strategy for Ireland 2002-2020: People, Places and Potential (2002), Dublin: Stationery Office.

UK National Statistics (2002a), *Regional Trends: GDP by NUTS 1, 2 and 3 Area: 1995-1998.* Available at www.statistics.gov.uk.

UK National Statistics (2002b), *Census of Employment: 1995-98.* Available from NOMIS (National Online Manpower Information Service) at www.nomisweb.co.uk.

UK National Statistics (2002c), *United Kingdom Input-Output Tables: 1995.* Available at www.statistics.gov.uk.

PART 2

Growth, Innovation and Irish Regional Development

Chapter 5

WHAT SHOULD IRISH POLICYMAKERS LEARN FROM RECENT ADVANCES IN GROWTH THEORY AND ECONOMIC GEOGRAPHY?

Edgar Morgenroth[1]

INTRODUCTION

During the last decade issues such as growth and convergence, core-periphery structures, and regional development have come to the forefront in policy circles. Within the EU, the Single Market project lead to a recognition that not all countries would benefit equally from the deepening of the EU (Braunerhjelm et al., 2000). Thus, the process of EU integration itself may lead to income divergences, which led the EU Commission to reform the Structural Funds and introduce the Cohesion Funds (see Cecchini, 1998). At the national level within Ireland there has also been renewed interest in the issue of Irish regional development from a policy perspective. Evidence for this can be found in the National Development Plan: 2000-2006 (2000), where for the first time, the government committed itself to the drawing up of a National Spatial Strategy: 2002-2020 (2002), which has since been published and which is to address the future spatial structure of Ireland. This concern about regional development emerged since, despite the exceptional perform-

---

[1] This paper is a shortened version of Morgenroth (2003a) and the reader is referred to that paper for a more detailed review.

ance of the national economy, at the regional level development during the 1990s was characterised by divergence between the Irish regions despite the fact that all regions grew
more rapidly than the EU average.

At the same time as political concerns about regional development increased, new theories of economic growth and economic geography were developed. The important innovation of
both literatures is that all results are derived from the actions of
individuals and firms in the market place in a general equilibrium setting. This means that these new models have the attractive property that they are rigorously derived and do not
ignore the implications of changes in one variable on the rest of
the economy. However, on the negative side, in order to make
the models mathematically tractable they require many simpli-
fications and in particular some restrictive assumptions regarding individual preferences and the cost functions facing firms
(see Neary, 2001).

Given that these new theoretical developments coincide
with a significant interest among policy makers in regional development issues, a natural question is to ask what policy lessons if any can be drawn from this new body of research and
such a review is the subject of this chapter. Indeed, the Irish
National Spatial Strategy (NSS) could have been considerably
improved if it had drawn on this large research literature[2].
However, given the many contributions to both literatures this
chapter can only aim to draw out the main findings on policy
rather than provide a thorough review of the complete literature. For more complete discussions of the new growth literature the reader is referred to books such as Hammond and
Roderiguez-Clare (1993), Aghion and Howitt (1998), or Barro
and Sala-i-Martin (1995), and for a review of the new economic
geography literature to Fujita, Krugman and Venables (1999),
Fujita and Thisse (2002) or Neary (2001).

An important point to note is that the literature reviewed in
this chapter is not the only approach to growth and spatial patterns of economic activity. Naturally, geographers also have

---

[2] See Morgenroth (2003b) for a critique of the National Spatial Strategy.

produced a large body of literature, and within economics alternative approaches such as evolutionary models, which are not covered here are also useful tools (see Hilliard and Jacobson in Chapter 8 of this volume). In general, it seems particularly appropriate for economists to study the geographical location of economic activity, and the resulting geographical patterns of agglomeration and dispersion, since it is the allocation of scarce resources through human interaction that determines the economy and therefore economic geography. Economics is the study of how scarce resources are allocated, not just across individuals and time, but also space.

NEW GROWTH THEORY

The major shortcoming of the older literature on economic growth was the fact that technical progress, which is the ultimate source of growth, could not be modelled and was therefore taken to be exogenous. Thus, the long run growth rate in these models depends just on the rate of exogenous technical progress and/or population growth, which is also exogenous. Given the exogeneity of the engines of growth, policy could not alter the long-run steady state growth rates, rather it could only alter the transition path towards that long-run equilibrium. The role for policy makers was therefore confined to ensuring that markets work efficiently (an assumption of these models). An important implication of these models is that poor countries should grow faster than rich countries, that is, they should converge as long as they have the same steady stated. This would arise out of diminishing returns to capital. In other words, as economies accumulate capital, average product declines, thus countries starting at a lower level of capital should have higher growth rates.

The recent endogenous growth theory has addressed the shortcomings of the earlier pioneering literature. In particular it has focused on how the limitations of diminishing returns could be overcome. These models have investigated how the accumulation of reproducible factors such as infrastructure, human capital or knowledge/innovation or through specialisation, trade, financial intermediation and social capital can generate growth. Clearly, it is these factors together that account for differences in growth rates between countries and there are important complementarities between them. Thus, successful research and development (R&D) activities will require individuals with a high level of human capital. Similarly, people with a higher level of human capital more readily adopt innovations. However, it is difficult to incorporate all these factors into one model.

R&D/Knowledge

Technical progress is to a large extent driven by R&D. This has been incorporated into growth models as the accumulation of knowledge (e.g. Romer, 1986) or improvements in the quality of intermediate inputs (e.g. Aghion and Howitt, 1992, 1998). In the Romer model learning by doing results from the investment process which implies that the knowledge of the workforce is a function of the capital stock. Since the state of knowledge is embodied in capital it is in effect a public good available to all individual producers. Thus, investment by individual producers generate an externality through an increase in this public good, which gives rise to increasing returns at the aggregate economy wide level.

Romer (1990) goes further by dropping the assumption of perfect competition which cannot hold if knowledge/technology is a non-rival partially excludable good. In this model research is carried out by individuals with high human capital and the stock of human capital generates growth. In equilibrium there is not enough human capital. In another model (Ben-David and Loewy, 2000), the level of human capital in a country is determined by knowledge accumulation in that country and by knowledge accumulation in other countries. The impact of "foreign" knowledge accumulation on the domestic economy depends on the ability of the domestic economy to access this knowledge which is determined by trade. Higher levels of trade result in higher growth rates since this increases the spillover (externality) from foreign knowledge. The model predicts conditional convergence among countries that trade extensively with one another.

Infrastructure

One avenue that has been explored is the effect of public infrastructure, which is typically modelled as an additional input in the production function (Barro, 1990; Futagami et al., 1993). Public infrastructure raises the marginal product of private capital thus sustaining growth. However, it is important to note that infrastructure has to be financed through taxes and it is therefore important that the tax revenue is spent on infrastructure that is more productive than any other expenditure that could have been financed by the tax take. Another important way in which infrastructure impacts on economies is by connecting them. Thus, Kelly (1997) argued along Smithian lines that infrastructure allows for an expansion of markets which in turn increases specialisation, which improves efficiency and therefore growth. Another way in which infrastructure has been incorporated into growth models is to assume that infrastructure reduces the cost of intermediate inputs by fostering specialisation (Bougheas, Demetriades and Mamuneas, 2000). This model yields a non-monotonic relationship between infrastructure and long-run growth. An important finding is that infrastructure accumulation is very productive if the tax rate is low and counter-productive if the tax rate is too high.

Human Capital

The role of human capital is a vital field of research since human capital can be viewed as an essential prerequisite to the adoption of the types of change induced by globalisation and new technologies. Human capital has been integrated into growth models in different ways and thus this literature is particularly rich in that it also provides interesting empirical test of the different models.

Human capital can be acquired through education, learning-by-doing or be passed on between generations. However, a crucial distinction has been made between models where human capital is needed for R&D purposes (see Aghion and Howitt, 1992) and models where human capital enters directly in the production function (Lucas, 1988). The former approach implies that growth is driven by the stock of human capital whereas the latter implies that growth is driven by the process of accumulation of human capital (see Aghion and Howitt, 1998). The Lucas approach assumes that the marginal product of human capital remains positive regardless of the state of technology, which is unrealistic. On the other hand, the Aghion and Howitt approach incorporates scale effects that suggest that large countries should grow faster since, other things being equal, large countries possess a larger stock of human capital, which is not supported by the data (see Jones, 1995; Cannon, 2000).

Finance

An important factor in the development of firms is the role of financial intermediation (see the review by Pagano, 1993). Interest rates can have a negative impact on investment in R&D and thus reduce growth. However, there are other ways in which financial intermediation can impact on growth. For example, the way in which savings are transformed into investment depend on the financial intermediaries. If these are inefficient or work in a non-competitive environment this can lead to less funding being made available for investment, since in this case the financial intermediaries may increase their margins. Government policy through the imposition of high reserve requirements, taxes or other regulation can also significantly reduce the fraction of savings that is funnelled into investment. Another way in which financial intermediaries have an important bearing on growth is through the allocation of capital. If they allocate resources to inefficient companies only, then growth is likely to be lower than if they allocated the capital to highly efficient firms. Clearly the allocation decisions are also subject to risk, thus the investments with the higher potential return also are often those with the higher risk. In general, financial intermediaries through their portfolio can hedge the risk better than individuals, which implies that the more risky but potentially more productive investment is more likely to be undertaken by financial intermediaries (Greenwood and Jovanovich, 1990; King and Levine, 1993).

Trade/Openness/Integration

In a number of the models highlighted above the degree of specialisation and the size of the market were the drivers of growth. Clearly, trade allows firms access to larger markets that their own domestic market and this may also therefore drive growth. Rivera-Batiz and Romer (1991) show in a simple model that if the mechanism that generates growth, e.g. R&D, is subject of increasing returns to scale then integration by increasing the extent of the market will lead to growth. Along similar lines, trade allows for a transfer of technology, which should lead to higher growth in countries that lag behind in terms of technological development. However, in models where such spillovers are limited geographically the general result is that the trade pattern after integration will be determined by initial conditions. Thus countries that are ahead in their technological development end up dominating the market in these high-tech sectors and will grow faster, despite the fact that trade is welfare improving in all countries. A further implication of being locked into the low-tech sectors is that the returns to education drop and therefore the incentives for individuals to gain higher levels of education decline thus reinforcing the lagging nature of that economy (Saarenheimo, 1993). However, government policy in the form of R&D subsidies can help change this outcome and allow a lagging country to become dominant in the high-tech sector (Grossman and Helpman, 1991).

The analysis of further expansion of a common market has also been investigated by Walz (1998). He showed that the integration of a technologically lagging country through trade liberalisation increases overall growth in the common market due to a reallocation of resources resulting from increased competition. However, workers in the high-tech sectors of the existing members are likely to see a decline in their relative wage and thus these workers lose out.

Social Capital

Finally, it is clear that the context in which individuals make decisions is an important determinant of the type of investment decision that will be made. Thus, the institutional framework, the rule of law, absence of corruption, the existence of trust among individuals etc., which might be summarised by the term social capital, are also important. While social capital is more difficult to incorporate into conventional mathematical growth models, this has not precluded economic research in this area. For example in a recent paper Zak and Knack (2001) develop a general equilibrium growth model where individuals face moral hazard problems. They show that in an environment where there is little trust investment will be lower which will reduce growth. In this literature social capital affects the development of all other types of capital mentioned above. Overall there appears to be empirical support for the notion that social capital matters (see Knack and Keefer, 1997; Zak and Knack, 2001; Hall and Jones, 1999).

NEW ECONOMIC GEOGRAPHY

Within the economics profession space has been one of the most neglected aspects in human interaction and economic development. This is perhaps surprising especially since early economists like Marshall, Cournot, Christaller, Lösch etc. did recognise the importance of geography. The new economic geography is not limited to the writings of Paul Krugman (1980, 1991), rather it is fast becoming a wider field which also incorporates geography into traditional models of trade.

The central aim of this literature is to explain how the economic geography, that is the degree of agglomeration and dispersion of economic activity and people come about. Thus, it aims not simply at description of the economic geography, nor does it aim to explain the development of one small-scale location by focusing on the characteristics, which distinguish such a region from other regions. Rather it attempts to distil out the major processes that are important in the development of the economic geography of all regions. Once one can explain how the spatial economies come into existence and operate one can progress to prediction and policy analysis. A description of the spatial patterns that are apparent is not enough to do policy analysis since it will not yield sufficient information on how the spatial pattern came into existence and therefore how policy can change the behaviour that will then change the spatial pattern. Similarly a description will not be much use for prediction since it captures a point in time only. Even if such a description covers a period of time, the lack of a rigorously developed behavioural foundation, would seriously limit the ability to forecast as this would have to be based on simple extrapolation, rather than taking into account the behaviour and expectations of individuals.

As will be seen this new literature incorporates some old ideas into models that utilise some advances in modelling techniques. It thus allows for a rigorous analysis using the language of logic. This approach yields testable models that generalise the development of economies in space which allow a focus on the important aspects by disregarding the less important ones.

Core Periphery

The basic new economic geography models have evolved from the new trade literature which was also importantly influenced by Krugman (e.g. Krugman, 1980 and Brander and Krugman, 1983). In his 1980 paper Krugman developed a model which incorporates economies of scale, product differentiation and imperfect competition. The production is subject to a fixed cost and a constant marginal cost, which implies that average cost declines at a diminishing rate at all output levels. In this model trade takes place due to increasing returns and each good will only be produced in one country by one firm and the gains from trade arise in the form of greater product diversity than would be produced in the autarkic situation. Thus, the increasing returns are pecuniary external returns to scale that arise out of the increase in the variety of goods, rather than returns to scale that arise out of spillovers (e.g. technology).

The introduction of transport costs of the "iceberg" variety results in different prices being charged for the goods in different countries, since transport costs only apply to international trade. The important result from the introduction of transport costs into this model is that countries will export the goods for which there is a large domestic demand — the home market effect. A larger domestic market allows firms to produce at a lower cost which means that their exports are also cheaper after transport costs have been added than when domestic demand is low. This also implies that the workers in the large country are better off since they face a lower price for consumption goods. Thus, the assumption of increasing returns in conjunction with transport costs gives rise to a home market effect.

Krugman (1991) extends this framework of increasing returns and transport costs in a model of two regions where there are two sectors, one being agriculture. Agricultural workers who are immobile produce the agricultural output while the manufacturing workers are fully mobile. In this model the transportation of agricultural goods is not subject to transport costs but that of manufacturing products does incur transport costs. The number of products that are produced in each region are proportional to the number of workers resident in them. Again the model gives rise to a home market effect but a second "competition effect" implies that manufacturing workers who live in a less populated region face less competition in the local market, which to some extent outweighs the benefit of locating in the larger market.

Once workers are allowed to migrate between regions an interesting result is obtained. Workers choose to locate where their real wage is highest and this has an implication for the mobility of workers and the concentration of manufacturing firms. Thus, if transport costs are high, the share of manufacturing is small or if returns to scale are small then the manufacturing firms will be distributed according to the distribution of agricultural workers. However, if the converse is the case then manufacturing firms will concentrate in that region which has a higher starting population. This is due to the fact that a slightly higher population in the home market reduces the cost of manufactured products in that region which will be reinforced through immigration. For example, if transport costs are low, a region with a slightly higher starting population will attract manufacturing firms due to increasing returns provided they are sufficient to outweigh the transport costs incurred in serving the smaller market. This will also result in lower prices for consumption goods in that region which will attract more workers which further reinforces the agglomeration process.

Hanson (1996) presents some empirical evidence showing that, following the signing of the North American Free Trade Agreement, manufacturing firms relocated from Mexico City to the Mexico-US frontier. Furthermore, there is some evidence for the EU that specialisation is increasing (Amiti, 1998). This story signals that there may be a danger for some countries from the EU policy on infrastructural investment to reduce transport costs, since, over a certain range of values for these costs, improved access to the core may actually hurt rather than help industry located in the periphery. However, this result is dependent on the importance of transport costs at a sectoral level. Industries which face low or negligible transport costs may prefer to locate in peripheral countries provided that there are other cost advantages. This may explain why Ireland has been so successful in attracting firms in the high-tech computer sector.

Firm location can also be affected by the presence of intellectual or human capital, which is closely related to R&D, and this is particularly true for high-tech industries. A study of the growth and location of the American biotechnology industry found that intellectual human capital flourishes in proximity to universities (see Zucker et al., 1998). Furthermore, the knowledge spillovers from intellectual human capital are spatially restricted and thus create agglomeration economies (Audretsch, 1998). Both of these factors impact on regional development within a country by restricting the number of locations at which innovative activity flourishes and by limiting the spillovers to a smaller geographical area. Notably these types of spillovers are not part of the new economic geography literature.

Spillovers in general seem to be spatially limited and it has been shown, using data for European regions, that a region's economic performance is related to the performance of its neighbouring regions (see Quah, 1996). Thus, spatial spillovers matter more than national characteristics in explaining income inequalities. This implies that the regional development potential is determined by the characteristics of the region and its neighbouring regions. Biehl (1991) argues that the crucial characteristics that determine a region's development potential are infrastructure, location, agglomeration and sectoral structure. Clearly, location cannot be changed and agglomeration and sectoral structure can only be changed over the longer term. Thus, infrastructure represents the only direct instrument of government policy for regional development. Infrastructure, by improving access and the general production environment, can help in attracting outside investment and foster domestic firms. However, the provision of infrastructure needs to be considered together with the other regional development determinants and in particular agglomeration economies. Infrastructure on its own will help a region develop and it is important to target infrastructure investment to specific nodes — towns and cities — where agglomeration economies are more likely to exist and where the industrial structure is more developed.

City Formation, City Growth and Urban Hierarchies

Given that these new models are capable of generating concentrations of economic activity, and obvious extension to the models might be to investigate whether they can also generate the emergence of cities, and if so whether special patterns in the distribution of cities emerge.

One attempt is the so-called racetrack economy, where the standard new economy geography model is extended by assuming that locations are evenly spread around a circumference (Fujita, Krugman and Venables, 1999). Starting with an even distribution of manufacturing, if this is not an equilibrium, (i.e. there are forces that generate a relocation of workers or firms), then the economy will move towards a pattern of agglomeration. Of course since transport costs are crucial in this model the agglomerated locations will be spread evenly around the circumference, with the number decreasing with decreasing transport costs which thus also induce a longer distance between locations.

This model has been further extended by assuming that rather than being located on a circumference, the locations are located on an infinite line. In this case the initial position is one with just one agglomeration of population, i.e. one city. In contrast to the other models here, labour can switch between uses from low-tech to high-tech which implies that both sectors will have to pay the same wage. With one agglomeration only this will also be the location where industry will locate. What is interesting is that when the population is allowed to grow new cities will emerge. This model shows that population growth results in a move from a monocentric to a policentric urban structure. With the further extension of many industries an urban hierarchy results in which one contains firms from all sectors while the others only contain a selection of sectors.

Agglomeration and Growth

Of course if agglomeration economies exist, these can also impact on the growth performance of regions. Martin and Ottaviano (2001) incorporate this type of mechanism into a growth model. They show that growth and agglomeration are mutually self-reinforcing. Thus, growth increases agglomeration and agglomeration increases growth. The model also shows that due to the continuous creation of new firms some firms re-locate to peripheral regions. Another contribution along these lines is that of Baldwin and Forslid (2000). They show that growth leads to agglomeration but that knowledge spillovers lead to dispersal of industry. In their model integration through a reduction in transactions costs for goods trade leads to increased concentration while integration that leads to a freer flow of ideas leads to dispersal. Another important finding of this model is that agglomeration not only maximises total growth globally but also raises growth for all regions, which reduces the negative impact of increased agglomeration.

WHAT ARE THE POLICY IMPLICATIONS?

In the two sections on endogenous growth theory and new economic geography policy implications were not explicitly highlighted. However, the usefulness of these models will ultimately be measured by their success in explaining the observed patterns of growth, convergence and the spatial distribution of economic activity and by their success in guiding policy. By summarising the policy implications of these models one also isolates issues that have yet to be addressed.

The most fundamental policy implication of the models discussed above is that one needs to understand the mechanisms that determine growth and the location of economic activity. This is quite distinct from simple and sometimes even simplistic descriptive approaches. That is not say that description is not a valuable exercise, but it cannot yield robust results for policy makers. This is especially true if the descriptive studies lack theory as is highlighted in the following quote, from Einstein: "It is quite wrong to try founding a theory on observable magnitudes alone. It is the theory which decides what we can observe" (Heisenberg, 1971).

With regard to the endogenous growth theory a number of important implications emerge. Firstly, almost all models incorporate some kind of externality or spillover, which generates additional growth through their public good nature. As is well known from the theory of public goods, these are rarely provided at their most efficient level through the market. The presence of externalities and spillovers therefore also implies that the engines of growth tend not to be provided at the optimal level. This market failure means that there is an important role for government to ensure that the engines of growth are supplied at the optimal level. This can be achieved through regulation or may require direct action by government, such as subsidies or the public provision of educations and infrastructure. This stands in contrast to the older growth literature in which the role of government was to merely ensure that markets were working competitively. However, an important implication of these new models is that convergence is no longer guaranteed, and that policy has long-lasting effects. This of course also applies to bad policies.

At a time when there is a debate about EU expansion and further integration, it is worth noting that integration is predicted to enhance growth. This is of course consistent with the experience of previous enlargements. Integration and trade are always welfare-improving in aggregate, but may require additional policy responses. Thus, countries that join a customs union with a poor industrial structure may not be able to fully benefit from membership even though they are better off with trade and integration.

The major contribution of the new economic geography is that it shows that concentration and the emergence of cities is a natural outcome of market interaction, if centripetal forces exceed the centrifugal forces. Empirically we see an increase in urbanisation, particularly at a time when the economy has changed to a high-tech economy. It is likely that such centripetal forces are therefore more important to high-tech industries, and indeed if these were diminished through policy such industries may well relocate to places where there are no such constraints. Of course government policy is unlikely to undermine these powerful market forces. Therefore, regional development policies should be centre-based, encouraging selected centres in conjunction with their respective hinterlands. In this respect the results of the endogenous growth theory are particularly pertinent.

A word of warning regarding concentration is nevertheless warranted. Even if centripetal forces are vital, over-concentration into one urban centre due to the inability, for whatever reason, of others to develop is likely to be damaging to growth. Henderson (2000) shows that over-concentration of the population in one urban centre reduces growth. Indeed, he points to Dublin as one example of a city that is too large relative to the overall size of the population of the country within which it is located. This raises an important question for policy makers about the optimal level of concentration/dispersal.

A further drawback of the new economic geography approach is that it relies on transport costs. Some researchers argue that these have been decreasing rapidly and should therefore not play such an important role. However, the rate of decrease in transport costs is not dramatic. Another issue that is likely to be important is the fact that non-pecuniary economies of scale are ignored in the new literature. Thus, this literature does need to develop further in order to provide a general explanation of the economic geography of the world.

CONCLUSION

This chapter has provided a brief non-technical review of the recent literature on economic growth and new economic geography. A thorough review of these literatures is clearly beyond the scope of this chapter and the reader is referred to some of the excellent reviews that have been published. However, these are often aimed at an academic audience and hence fail to draw out the important policy conclusions, something this chapter has attempted to do. Clearly with the brevity of this review a lot of interesting findings have been ignored. Also in such a non-technical review it is difficult to draw out some of the advances that have been made in the new literature. However, it is hoped some of the flavour of these extensive literatures has been conveyed.

Among the major contributions of these fields of research is the fact that they give firm theoretic foundations to phenomena that had often been described but the mechanisms of their emergence had not been properly modelled. Importantly this moves away from simply asserting that these mechanisms are responsible to proving that they really could. This then also allows the full implications of policy to be analysed. For example, in the endogenous growth models infrastructure has been included as a driver of growth. This may seem obvious. But it is not that obvious that infrastructure which has to be financed through taxes has the biggest positive impact if tax rates are low. Such an analysis is not possible without rigorous models. Of course this also implies that without knowledge of the mechanisms tax policy could be erroneous.

The important lesson of this is that policymakers should focus their attention at studies that aim to uncover the reasons for certain phenomena rather than those that simply describe them. Given the complexity of the factors that impinge on regional development this would seem to be particularly important with regard to policies such as the National Development Plan: 2000-2006) (2000) and the National Spatial Strategy: 2002-2020 (2002).

References

Aghion, P. and Howitt, P. (1992), "A Model of Growth through Creative Destruction", *Econometrica*, Vol. 60, No. 2, 323-351.

Aghion, P. and Howitt, P. (1998), *Endogenous Growth Theory*, Cambridge (MA): MIT Press.

Amiti, M. (1998), "New Trade Theory and Industrial Location n the EU: A Survey of the Evidence", *Oxford Review of Economic Policy*, Vol. 14, No. 2, 45-53.

Audretsch, A.J. (1998), "Agglomeration and the Location of Innovative Activity", *Oxford Review of Economic Policy*, Vol. 14, No. 2, 18-29.

Baldwin, R.E and Forslid, R. (2000), "The Core-Periphery Model and Endogenous Growth: Stabilising and Destabilising Integration", *Economica*, Vol. 67, No. 267, 307-324.

Barro, R.J. (1990), "Government Spending in a Simple Model of Endogenous Growth," *Journal of Political Economy*, Vol. 98, No. 5, 103-26.

Barro, R. and Sala-i-Martin, X. (1995), *Economic Growth*, New York, McGraw Hill.

Ben-David, D. and Loewy, M.B. (2000), "Knowledge Dissemination, Capital Accumulation, Trade, and Endogenous Growth", *Oxford Economic Papers,* 52, No. 4, 637-50.

Biehl, D. (1991), "The Role of Infrastructure in Economic Development", In R. Vickerman (ed.) *Infrastructure and Regional Development,* London: Pion Ltd. pp. 36-50.

Bougheas, S., Demetriades, P.O. and Mamuneas, T. (2000), "Infrastructure, Specialisation and Economic Growth." *Canadian Journal of Economics,* Vol. 33, No. 2, 506-522.

Brander, J. and P. Krugman (1983), "A 'Reciprocal Dumping' Model of International Trade", *Journal of International Economics*, Vol. 15, 313-321.

Braunerhjelm, P., Faini, R., Norman, V., Ruane, F. and Seabright, P. (2000), *Integration and the Regions of Europe: How the Right Policies Can Prevent Polarization.* Monitoring European Integration 10. London: Centre for Economic Policy Research.

Cannon, E. (2000), "Human Capital: Level versus Growth Effects," *Oxford Economic Papers*, Vol. 52, No. 4, 670-76.

Cecchini, P. (1998), *The European Challenge 1992: The Benefits of the Single Market.* Aldershot: Wildwood House.

Fujita, M., Krugman, P.A. and Venables, A.J. (1999), *The Spatial Economy: Cities, Regions and International Trade*. Cambridge, MA: MIT Press

Fujita, M. and Thisse, J-F. (2002), *Economics of Agglomeration: Cities, Industrial Location and Regional Growth*. Cambridge: Cambridge University Press.

Futagami, K., Morita, Y. and Shibata, A. (1993), "Dynamic Analysis of an Endogenous Growth Model with Public Capital," *Scandinavian Journal of Economics*, Vol. 95, No. 4, 607-625.

Greenwood, J. and Jovanovic, B. (1990), "Financial Development, Growth and the Distribution of Income", *Journal of Political Economy*, Vol. 98, No. 5, 1076-1107.

Grossman, G. M. and Helpman, E. (1991), *Innovation and Growth in the Global Economy*. Cambridge MA: MIT Press.

Hall, R.E. and Jones, C.I. (1999), "Why Do Some Countries Produce so Much More Output per Worker than Others?", *Quarterly Journal of Economics*, Vol. 114, No. 1, 83-116.

Hammond, P. J. and Rodriguez-Clare, A. (1993), "On Endogenising Long-run Growth", *Scandinavian Journal of Economics*, Vol. 95, No. 4, 391-426.

Hanson, G. (1996), "Economic Integration, Intraindustry Trade, and Frontier Regions", *European Economic Review*. Vol. 40, No.3-5, 941-49

Heisenberg, W. (1971), *Physics and Beyond: Encounters and Conversations*. New York: Harper and Row.

Henderson, V. (2000), "The Effects of Urban Concentration on Growth", *National Bureau of Economic Research Working Paper*, No. 7503.

Jones, C.I. (1995), "R&D-Based Models of Economic Growth", *Journal of Political Economy*. Vol. 103, No. 4, 759-784.

Kelly, M. (1997), "The Dynamics of Smithian Growth", *Quarterly Journal of Economics*, Vol. 112, No. 3, 939-964.

King, R.G. and Levine, R. (1993), "Finance, Entrepreneurship and Growth: Theory and Evidence", *Journal of Monetary Economics*, Vol. 32, No. 3, 513-542.

Knack, S. and Keefer, P. (1997), "Does Social Capital have an Economic Payoff?", *Quarterly Journal of Economics*, Vol. 112, No. 4, 1252-1288.

Krugman, P. (1980), "Scale Economies, Product Differentiation, and the Pattern of Trade", *American Economic Review*, Vol. 70, 950-959.

Krugman, P.A. (1991), "Increasing Returns and Economic Geography", *Journal of Political Economy*, Vol. 99, No. 3, 483-99.

Lucas, R. (1988), "On the Mechanics of Economic Development", *Journal of Monetary Economics*, Vol. 22, No. 1, pp. 3-42.

Martin, P. and Ottaviano, G. (2001), "Growth and Agglomeration", *International Economic Review*, Vol. 42, No. 4, 947-968.

Morgenroth, E. (2003a), "What Should Policy Makers Learn From Recent Advances in Growth Theory and Economic Geography?" *ESRI Working Paper*, No 150.

Morgenroth, E. (2003b), "A Critical Assessment of the National Spatial Strategy", ESRI Seminar Paper, February.

National Development Plan: 2000-2006 (2000), Dublin: Stationery Office

National Development Strategy: 2002-2020: People, Places and Potential (2002), Dublin: Stationery Office

Neary, J. P. (2001), "Of Hype and Hyperbolas: Introducing the New Economic Geography", *Journal of Economic Literature*, Vol. 39, No. 2, 536-561.

Pagano, M. (1993), "Financial markets and Growth: An Overview", *European Economic Review*, Vol. 37, No. 2-3, 613-622.

Quah, D. (1996), "Regional Convergence Clusters Across Europe", *European Economic Review*, Vol. 4, No. 4-5, 951-958.

Rivera-Batiz, L.A. and Romer, P.M. (1991), "Economic Integration and Endogenous Growth", *Quarterly Journal of Economics*, Vol. 106, No. 2, 531-555.

Romer, P.M. (1986), "Increasing Returns and Long-run Growth", *Journal of Political Economy*, Vol. 94, No. 5, 1002-37.

Romer, P.M. (1990), "Endogenous Technological Change", *Journal of Political Economy*, Vol. 98, No. 2, 71-102.

Saarenheimo, T. (1993), "Trade, Human Capital Accumulation and Growth in an Underdeveloped Economy", *Scandinavian Journal of Economics*, Vol. 95, No. 4, 535-557.

Walz, U. (1998), "Does an Enlargement of a Common Market Stimulate Growth and Convergence?", *Journal of International Economics*, Vol. 45, No. 2, 297-321.

Zak, P.J. and Knack, S. (2001), "Trust and Growth", *Economic Journal*, Vol. 111, No. 470, 295-321.

Zucker, L., Darby, M. and Brewer, M. (1998), "Intellectual Human Capital and the Birth of U.S. Biotechnology Enterprises", *American Economic Review*, Vol. 88, No. 1, 290-306.

Chapter 6

RESEARCH AND DEVELOPMENT CENTRES IN LESS FAVOURED REGIONS: TOWARDS AN *EX ANTE* IMPACT ASSESSMENT

Stephen Roper, Nola Hewitt-Dundas and James H. Love

INTRODUCTION

The capability of a region to generate advanced technology, information and ultimately knowledge is regarded as the single most important force driving the secular process of economic growth. In particular, regional investment in research and development (R&D), technological development and innovation is perceived as being strongly associated with productivity, growth and sustained international competitiveness (Malecki, 1981; Romer, 1990; Eaton and Kortum, 1996). Moreover, as Audretsch (1998, p. 26) argues, "knowledge spillovers tend to be spatially restricted. . . . The increased importance of innovative activity in the leading developed countries has triggered a resurgence in the importance of local regions as a key source of comparative advantage".

Alongside the importance of knowledge as a driver of economic growth, recent research has emphasised the particular characteristics of knowledge production as (a) exhibiting increasing returns, and (b) having the potential for strongly localised benefits. Such agglomeration advantages will tend to *increase* economic disparities between knowledge-rich ("core") and knowledge-poor ("lagging") regions. For development agencies and governments in less favoured regions (LFRs), and for supra-regional and supra-national organisations (e.g. the EU) concerned with inter-regional cohesion, counteracting this centralising tendency, represents a massive strategic and policy challenge. How, for example, do you cost effectively stimulate technological development capability in LFRs and establish a positive developmental trajectory?

Even a casual survey suggests a kaleidoscopic range of answers. National policies have varied from the Irish policy of establishing and maintaining the fiscal and labour market conditions necessary to attract inward investment to Scandinavian and Israeli approaches which have sought technological self-sufficiency by massive investments in domestic R&D capability and their national innovation systems (e.g. Roper and Frenkel, 2000; Roper, 2001). Similarly, regional strategies have also varied substantially from approaches based on physical planning such as the growth pole strategies of some French regions to "softer", network-based, approaches such as that adopted in Wales. Other regions have sought to develop new dynamics based on the development of new regional relationships such as that surrounding the Øresund Bridge between Sweden and Denmark.

A common element of each type of strategy, however, has been the provision of public support for R&D investment, often justified by arguments related to market failure (e.g. Metcalfe, 1997).[1] Grants or loans, for example, may enable firms to undertake R&D or innovation projects, which would otherwise be too risky or unviable and so develop capabilities with long-term competitive benefits. Public support may also enable universities to establish Centres of Excellence providing knowledge creation or assimilation services for local companies. Along with this public support, has gone an increasing emphasis on the *ex post* evaluation of R&D projects' downstream and long-term effects. Our argument here is that these *ex post* studies now constitute a knowledge base, which is sufficiently broad to form *ex*

---

[1] More strategic arguments for public intervention also exist, however, reflecting the importance of the policy and institutional infrastructure in the effectiveness of the regional innovation system, and the potential importance of public support for regions' technological development (e.g. Cooke et al., 2002).

ante judgements on the likely effects of specific R&D projects in varying geographical and economic settings. In what follows, we focus on one specific case, that of a prospective R&D centre intended to be located in a less favoured region (or LFR).

We begin in the next section by outlining our conceptual approach. This has two basic elements relating first to an assessment of the global benefits of any R&D project, and secondly to the share of those benefits accruing to the LFR.

GLOBAL BENEFITS AND LOCAL SHARES

R&D activity includes *research*, i.e. all systematic work to increase the stock of knowledge, including knowledge of the behaviour of the material and physical universe, and of man, culture and society, and *development*, i.e. all systematic work to devise novel ways of using this increased stock of knowledge. R&D generates distinct "private" and "social" returns each of which may occur through a number of different mechanisms. Thus the total global benefits (TB) of an R&D project may be summarised by:

$$TB = \sum_i PB_i + \sum_j SB_j \qquad (1)$$

where PB_i are private benefits of type i and SB_j are social benefits of type j. Private returns accrue to the organisation conducting the R&D (i.e. the company or university), with the most obvious "private" return being the addition to the (private) stock or reservoir of knowledge from the R&D. This may lead to commercial applications or the sale of licenses to other technology users.

The wider social benefits derived from R&D activity depend on the extent of "spillovers", (positive) externalities, or economies of localisation.[2] In each case the basic idea is that there are

---

[2] The existence of these potential positive externalities from R&D drives a wedge between the private return and the social return, raising the social rate of return for R&D above the private rate of return. Indeed, the empirical literature demonstrates that the social rate of return from privately funded R&D is several times higher than the private rate of return (Cohen and Levin, 1989; Griliches 1979, 1991; Nadiri, 1980, 1993). Firms unable to appropriate all of the benefits of their R&D investments, therefore under-invest in R&D relative to the social optimum (Nelson, 1959; Arrow, 1962; Dasgupta and David, 1994). This market failure is often used to justify public support for R&D activity with

certain advantages which firms derive from being in close geographical proximity to an R&D centre in the same or a related sector. Two main types of externality are commonly identified: *rent
(or pecuniary)* externalities, which are the result of market transactions; and *pure knowledge spillovers* which are independent of any
market mechanism (Griliches, 1979, 1992). Beugelsdijk and Cornet (2001, p. 3) summarise the distinction as follows:

> Rent spillovers arise when quality improvements by a sup-
> plier are not fully translated into higher prices for the
> buyer(s). Productivity gains are then recorded in a differ-
> ent firm or industry than the one that generated the pro-
> ductivity gains in the first place. Rent spillovers occur in
> input-output relations. Pure knowledge spillovers refer to
> the impact of the discovered ideas or compounds on the
> productivity of the research endeavours of others. Pure
> knowledge spillovers are benefits of innovative activities
> of one firm that accrue to another without following market
> transactions.

Pure knowledge spillovers do not require this type of "market"
interaction but depend instead on the free flow of knowledge
from the R&D centre and its absorption and adoption by other
local organisations. For example:

> Positive externalities of scientific discoveries on the pro-
> ductivity of firms which neither made the discovery
> themselves nor licensed its use from the holder of intel-
> lectual property rights (Zucker et al, 1998a, p. 65).

> A prototypical externality, by which one or a few agents
> investing in research or technology development will
> end up facilitating other agents' innovation efforts (either
> unintentionally, as it happens when inventions are imi-
> tated, or intentionally, as it may happen when scientists
> divulge the results of their research) (Breschi and Lis-
> soni, 2001, p. 975).

The second issue which arises from equation 1 are the types of
private and social benefits (i.e. the i and j) which arise from R&D.

---

the aim of raising the level of R&D investment above the privately optimal
level and bringing it closer to the social optimum (e.g. Metcalfe, 1997).

One of the most effective approaches to this issue has been developed by the Health Economics Research Group (HERG) at Brunel University (e.g. Buxton and Hanney, 1994, 1996, 1997; Hanney et al., 2000). Their approach — oriented towards wholly publicly funded health research units — outlines an inventory of the benefits that might stem from a publicly supported R&D centre. Generalising their approach somewhat, we can define a set of potential public and private benefits which might stem from any R&D centre.[3] The resulting 8-category inventory of global benefits expected from an R&D project is summarised in Table 6.1.

For a host region, however, what is important is not so much the global benefit of an R&D project but the share of that benefit accruing to the region itself. This regional benefit (RB) may be expressed as:

$$RB = \sum_i \gamma_i^P PB_i + \sum_j \gamma_j^S SB_j \qquad (2)$$

where γ_i^P and γ_i^S are the regional shares of the private and social benefits of R&D respectively (which might be expected to be different for different regions). For example, larger regions or those with more receptive firms, might derive greater advantages from the presence of a new R&D facility than smaller regions or those with less technologically sophisticated firms.

The remainder of the chapter focuses on the two issues reflected in equations (1) and (2). Section 3 examines the total global benefits which might arise from an R&D centre, examining separately private and social returns. Section 4 then examines the factors which determine an LFR's share of these global benefits. These turn out to depend not only on the characteristics of the LFR itself but also on the characteristics of the R&D centre, and on the "synergy" between the R&D centre and the economy of the LFR.

---

[3] We generalise the HERG typology in three main areas. First we distinguish between private and public (or social) benefits. Second, we adopt a generalised treatment of downstream effects taking into account potential commercial, industrial and fiscal benefits and, thirdly, we make some development to the "broader economic benefits" category to reflect potential spillovers.

Table 6.1: Inventory of Public and Private Categories of Payback from Research Activity

A Private Benefits	5.3 Staff development/educational benefits.
1. Increments to Knowledge	5.4 Increased capacity to use existing research findings, public
1.1 Basic R&D Results	
1.2 Applied R&D results	5.5 Reputational and halo effects, public
1.3 Developmental R&D results	
1.4 Other research results	5.6 Research clustering or agglomeration benefits
2. Benefits to Future Research and Research Use	**6. Political and Administrative Benefits**
2.1 Better targeting of future research	6.1 Improved information bases on which to take political and executive decisions
2.2 Staff development and education	
2.3 Better research management skills	6.2 Other political benefits from undertaking research.
2.4 Increased capacity to use existing research findings	**7. Rent or Market Spillovers**
2.5 Reputational and halo effects	7.1 Benefits of cost reductions in other organisations
3. Private Benefits from Commercial Application	7.2 Benefits of new improved products or services to other organisations
3.1 Cost reduction in existing products/services	7.3 Availability of pool of trained staff etc.
3.2 New or improved products or services	7.4 Partnership or network gains
3.3 Process or organisational improvement	7.5 Fiscal benefits of research and other activity
3.4 Reputational or strategic benefits	8. Pure knowledge Spillovers
3.5 Revenues gained from Intellectual Property Rights	**B. Wider Social and Public Benefits**
4. Increments to Knowledge	8.1 Intentional knowledge spillovers
4.1 Basic Research Results	8.2 Unintentional knowledge spillovers
4.2 Applied Research Results	
4.3 Developmental R&D results	8.3 Spin-outs etc
4.4 Other research results	8.4 Reputational, image or halo effects
5. Benefits to Future Research and Research Use:	8.5 Demonstration effects
5.1 Better targeting of future research, public	8.6 Agglomeration or informational advantages
5.2 Development of research skills, personnel and overall research capacity	

ASSESSING THE GLOBAL BENEFITS OF R&D PROJECTS

Private Benefits

In examining the private benefits from R&D it is important to distinguish between (a) those relating to increments to the stock of knowledge (reflecting the different types of R&D which might be undertaken), "learning" and subsequent benefits to future research or market position (Table 6.1, items 1.1–1.4 and 2.1-2.5), and (b) private benefits from commercial application (Table 6.1, items 3.1–3.5).

Research in Ireland, for example, has demonstrated that plants with an in-house R&D capability are more likely to be innovating (Roper and Hewitt-Dundas, 1998; Love and Roper, 2001), have higher turnover and employment growth, productivity and profitability (Roper and Hewitt-Dundas, 1998), have a longer life-span than similar plants with no in-house R&D capability (Ruane and Kearns, 2001) and sell a larger proportion of their output outside the UK and Irish markets (Roper and Love, 2001).

Other more organisational advantages may also be evident in terms of improvements in the firm's R&D capability. Research projects may, for example, enable subsequent projects to be better focussed or better managed, reducing costs or increasing the probability of success (Table 6.1, item 2.1). Research activity may also lead to developments in the human resources and managerial capacity of an R&D centre and therefore more positive outcomes in future research projects (Table 6.1, item 2.2). Other reputational and "halo" effects may also stem from having an R&D facility or having a reputation as an R&D active or innovative business (Table 6.1, item 2.5).[4] Potential employees may also find R&D active employers more appealing and development agencies may feel more comfortable if an otherwise mobile manufacturing operation has a (relatively immobile) R&D facility attached (Ruane and Kearns, 2001).

Undertaking R&D may also improve firms' ability to absorb R&D results or knowledge from elsewhere and manage collaborative R&D projects with other organisations. For example,

---

[4] For example, the brand images of 3M and HP are largely based on their capability as innovative firms.

Veugelers and Cassiman (1999) in their analysis of Belgian data suggest that firms undertaking in-house R&D benefited more from external information sources than companies which had no in-house R&D activity. Similarly, Love and Roper (2001) found that UK and German firms were obtaining economies of scope in the management of outsourced R&D. In other words, management competencies developed in outsourcing in one element of the product development process were being used to take advantage of the potential benefits of outsourcing in other activities (Table 6.1, item 2.4).

Although, by definition, these private benefits accrue to the organisation which is undertaking the R&D, the increasing globalisation of R&D activity may mean that the spatial distribution of the commercial benefits of R&D activity may be very different to that of the R&D activity itself. Reddy (1997, pp. 1821-22) summarises the situation as follows:

> Today, new needs or trends can arise in any advanced market and the latest technologies may be located in another. TNCs[5] attempt to gain a competitive advantage by sensing needs in one country, responding with capabilities located in a second, and diffusing the resulting innovation in markets world-wide.

Miotti et al. (2001), for example, note that among Korean multinationals FDI to the US has been partly motivated by technology sourcing in high-tech sectors whereas their investments in Europe are more concentrated on the development of manufacturing facilities for consumer electronics.

Rent Spillovers

Rent spillovers occur where an R&D centre generates either a local supply or demand in which either cost reductions or quality improvements are not fully reflected in price changes. This type of effect may be mediated through the supply chain, with positive effects on the R&D centre's suppliers and customers (Table 6.1, items 7.1 and 7.2), or factor-markets with positive

---

[5] Trans-national corporations.

effects on other local organisations with similar factor demands (Table 6.1, item 7.3). For an LFR, the extent of any supply-chain benefits will depend on the extent to which an R&D centre is embedded within the local economy, i.e. is sourcing locally and selling services and products to other local organisations. Relatively little is known about the embeddedness (or otherwise) of R&D centres in different regional settings, however, useful parallels can be drawn with the much better understood situation of high-tech, multi-national inward investment projects. Here, particularly within LFRs, the evidence suggests that projects are often only weakly embedded in the host region, limited by the restricted availability of the type of complex products and services demanded by high-tech firms (e.g. Turok, 1993; Crone and Roper, 2000). Local demand for the type of products or services offered by an R&D centre is also more likely to be weaker within an LFR than within a region with, say, a greater concentration of high-tech industry, again reducing the potential for localised spillovers through forward linkages.

Other forms of rent spillovers depend on the movement of research-trained staff who act as localised carriers of knowledge (Table 6.1, item 7.3). Where individuals are patent-holding scientists or engineers, or have the skills and know-how to engage in technological advance, local moves may generate localised knowledge spillovers. Some studies of this process have been conducted but these have tended to examine in detail a particular industrial sector, often located in a single geographical area. For example, Zucker et al. (1998a; 1998b) examined the role of "star" scientists in the development of the biotechnology industry in California. Using a version of the "knowledge production function" approach, Zucker et al. (1998a) consider how the innovation output (defined as products in development) of 78 biotechnology firms was affected by the number of relevant articles authored by identified star researchers within the firms' geographical region. The result is positive and significant. While this might at first sight appear to support the localised knowledge spillover concept, Zucker et al. go much further, and trace whether each star was directly in collaboration with a given firm at the time of each article's publication. When they separate out those stars which do and do not have direct links with enterprises, only the former are found to have a positive effect on new products in development. The publications of local stars with no company contacts have no effect on innovation. They conclude that the positive impact of research universities on nearby firms is not the result of localised knowledge spillovers, but arises mainly from identifiable market exchanges between individual university star scientists and the firms. These scientists act as conduits between universities and the companies with whom they are affiliated, but not to all companies. Thus to the extent that knowledge "spills over", it happens as a result of clear market mechanisms and only to those firms that pay for the expertise; this is quite different from the informal, face-to-face knowledge exchanges assumed by much of the knowledge spillover literature.[6]

It is hard to assess the significance of these results for LFRs save to say that within most LFRs opportunities for "stars" to move to another firm within the region will probably be relatively limited. Perhaps more important, however, is the possibility that the research training provided by R&D centres may enrich the local labour pool and help in the creation of a cohort of research trained staff which might find other employment locally.

Pure Knowledge Spillovers

The very nature of pure knowledge spillovers makes them particularly difficult to observe directly but it is often possible to observe their effects (Table 6.1, items 8.1-8.6). Audretsch (1998), for example, notes the strong statistical relationship between R&D inputs and innovation outputs at the level of coun-

---

[6] The knowledge flows identified by Zucker et al. (1998a) are therefore designed to exclude some firms, and cannot be regarded as a non-excludable quasi-public good benefiting all firms in a given area, in the sense of the "pure" knowledge spillover. This may indeed have a localised effect, but only because the stars prefer to have company links or engage in start-ups within commuting distance of the universities in which they retain their affiliation. Zucker *et al* therefore conclude that previous research on localised knowledge spillovers may have resulted form a serious specification error, in failing to control for the contractual relations of individual scientists with local firms.

tries and industrial sectors, but the less robust relationship at the level of the individual firm, especially when small firms are included in the analysis. This suggests that small firms, in particular, may derive their knowledge inputs not from their own R&D but from knowledge spillovers from other firms and from universities within the country or industrial sector (Table 6.1, items 8.1 and 8.2).

Empirical evidence on "pure" knowledge spillovers comes from a number of studies which have attempted to link levels of innovative activity in a region to indicators of academic research output or inputs. The pioneering work in this area is Jaffe (1989) on the "real effect" of academic research. Working at the level of US states, Jaffe found that the number of patents registered in any state for a given sector was a positive function not only of industrial R&D expenditure in the state but also of the amount of research expenditure by universities in the state (after allowing for differences in the absolute size of states). This is interpreted as indicating that knowledge generated at universities spills over into the industrial sector, leading to higher innovative output than would otherwise be the case. Very similar results for the French administrative regions are found by Piergiovanni and Santarelli (2001). Jaffe (1989) also looks at the causal links between industrial R&D and university research at the state level, and finds some evidence that the latter causes the former but not vice versa. "Thus a state that improves is university research system will increase local innovation both by attracting industrial R&D and by augmenting its productivity" (p. 968).

Using the same methodology, Acs et al. (1992) perform a similar study, but using a broader measure of innovation, i.e. the number of innovations registered with the US Small Business Administration. As before, they find that both corporate and university research expenditure has a positive effect on innovation levels, but estimate that the impact of university research is twice as great as that estimated by Jaffe, and that the geographical coincidence of university and corporate R&D had a positive effect on innovation (neither Jaffe nor Piergiovanni and Santarelli found such an effect). Acs et al. interpret their results as indicating that localised knowledge spillovers are more important than Jaffe had found.

In a later paper using similar data, Acs et al. (1994) find that while the innovation output of all firms rise with the amount of R&D inputs from corporations and universities in a given state, the former is especially important in providing knowledge inputs to the innovation of large firms, while the latter is more important to small firms' innovative output. They interpret this as suggesting that university research can substitute for in-house research among smaller firms, and suggest that small firms are especially adept at exploiting spillovers from university labs, while large firms are better at exploiting knowledge created in their own labs. This interpretation has been criticised by Breschi and Lissoni (2001), who argue that the results may simply show that *innovative* small firms may be readier than larger ones to subcontract their research projects to universities because they cannot afford in-house R&D, and are effectively forced to work with local institutions because they lack information about more distant (and possibly more efficient) universities.

Breschi and Lissoni also criticise the work of Jaffe (1989) and Acs et al. (1992; 1994) for operating at very aggregated levels of both spatial unit and technology. For example, it seems unlikely that US states are the appropriate area within which academics, inventors and entrepreneurs will have frequent face-to-face contact. In addition, Jaffe used very broad industry sectors (such as "electronics, optics and nuclear technology"), which Breschi and Lissoni argue are too wide to presume a match between, say, corporate R&D objectives and university expertise which could give rise to meaningful spillovers. Audretsch and Feldman (1996) attempt to deal with the second of these issues by employing more narrowly defined industrial sectors (4-digit SIC level), but again operating at the level of the US state. This paper examines the extent to which there is geographical clustering of innovative activity, even after allowing for the general spatial concentration of production. They find that there is a systematic tendency for innovations to cluster, and that this can be explained by three factors: the extent of industry R&D expenditure; the extent of skilled labour; and the pool of the science base as measured by university research expenditure. Audretsch and Feldman interpret this as supportive of a flow of tacit knowledge being transmitted through face-to-face contact. However, it should be noted that at least one of their explanatory variables (extent of skilled labour) is more appropriately considered as a Marshallian rent (or pecuniary) spillover, available to all firms within a given spatial/technological area through the workings of the market, rather than as a "pure" knowledge spillover.

The clearest attempt to look for knowledge spillovers at a more local scale is made by Anselin et al. (2000). Another American study, Anselin et al., operate at the Metropolitan Statistical Area (MSA) level, a level of spatial scale based around cities, and much smaller than the state level. Their results indicate that spillovers from university research do indeed have a positive impact on the levels of innovation within MSAs, and that this effect can extend beyond the boundary of the MSA up to 75 miles from the central city. Crucially, however, they find that this effect varies substantially across (2-digit) industrial sectors; for example, they find no spillover effect in chemicals and pharmaceuticals, but very strong and significant spillover effects in electronics and scientific instruments. (Jaffe, 1989, also finds that spillover effects vary significantly by industry sector.)

Almost all the analysis reviewed above is US-based, and all, to a greater or lesser extent, finds evidence of knowledge spillovers. There is, however, a series of research from the Netherlands which consistently fails to find similar effects. For example, Beugelsdijck and Cornet (2001) apply the knowledge production function concept to an analysis of Dutch manufacturing firms, relating the innovative output (i.e. share of new products as a proportion of turnover) of each firm to its own innovation expenditure, the innovation expenditure of firms within 1,2, and 3-digit postcode of the firm, and the location within a 2-digit postcode of a technical university. They find no evidence that innovation expenditures by nearby firms have a greater effect on a firm's innovative performance than expenditure by firms located further away. They do, however, find some evidence of positive spillovers from local technological universities. The difference between this result and the American studies may in part be due to differences in variable definitions, but the authors suggest it is more likely to be due to differences in scale: they point out that many of the US studies reviewed above regard proximity in terms of a two-hour train trip, which in the Netherlands will imply a journey into Belgium or Germany. "This study thus suggests that the Netherlands is too small a country to have proximity play the leading role in facilitating knowledge spillovers. *This conclusion might a fortiori hold for other regions of similar size*" (Beugelsdijck and Cornet, 2001, p. 17, emphasis added).

The results of Beugelsdijck and Cornet (2001) are salutary for the potential for pure knowledge spillovers in LFRs. Such regions might typically be characterised as having a lower absorptive capacity than most areas within the Netherlands and yet even here there is very little positive evidence of knowledge spillovers. In short therefore, while the US evidence clearly points to the potential for pure knowledge spillovers, their likely significance for LFRs — particularly spatially smaller units — is more doubtful. More important perhaps in such areas are rent based spillovers related either to the movements of "stars", local supply-chains or the creation of a skilled labour pool.

ASSESSING HOST REGION'S SHARE

In this section we consider the factors, which determine the share of these global benefits of any R&D project which might accrue to an LFR. We consider three main factors. First, we consider the profile of the R&D centre itself such as sector, size, ownership etc. For example, recent evidence from Guellec and van Pottlesberghe de la Potterie (2001), who analysed R&D and productivity growth in 16 OECD countries, suggests that a 1 per cent increase in business R&D generates a 0.13 per cent increase in productivity; a 1 per cent increase in foreign R&D generates a 0.44 per cent increase in productivity; and, a 1 per cent increase in public R&D generates a 0.17 per cent increase in productivity. The technological character of the R&D being conducted may also have an impact on the benefits which might be expected, with a range of studies suggesting that globally the social returns from basic or fundamental research are likely to be higher than those from more strategic or applied research activity (e.g. Jaffe et al., 1993).

Secondly, we focus on the economic landscape of the LFR, where sectoral composition, firm size, technological capability etc. will shape the capability of the host region to take advantage of potential knowledge spillovers. Recent studies such as that by Fernandez et al. (1996) on government supported R&D in Spain, for example, have suggested that for less developed regions or those with an intermediate technological and industrial base, the locally captured social returns might be greater from strategic or applied rather than basic research. Fernandez et al. (1996) also argue that the dominance of the Spanish economy by small and medium-sized firms, limits its capacity to appropriate locally the full benefits of publicly supported basic research activity. Finally, we focus on the importance of "synergy", the match between the characteristics of the R&D facility and the host LFR.

Profile of the R&D Centre

Perhaps the most important characteristic of an R&D centre in terms of determining the share of the benefits which will accrue within the region is the type of R&D being undertaken. For basic research, for example, where the knowledge generated is not specifically linked to any immediate market need, global spillovers are generally thought to be greatest. Here, social benefits arise from the production of skilled manpower and the "public good" nature of the research outputs, i.e. the results of pre-competitive research can be shared by a group of companies without reducing the incentives to develop products or processes. There may also be strategic benefits in conducting basic research. Smith (1989), for example, argues that public support for basic research is important if the fundamental science base of the country is to be sustained. Investments in basic research may also act as an attraction for both academic staff and high quality students to move to and remain within a region. Nonetheless, the links between basic research and economic development — particularly at a regional level — remain ill-defined and unpredictable. Hence, Smith (1989) argues that investment in this type of activity may be difficult to justify in the context of a slowly growing LFR facing tight budgetary constraints.

Applied R&D is directed at specific problems or possibilities but is not aimed at achieving direct practical application. From a public perspective this type of research generates knowledge and internal capability, which keeps firms, industry, and the public sector at the forefront of technological developments. The knowledge generated by applied research activity is likely to be more "specific", however, than that generated by basic research. This may limit the extent of any knowledge spillovers, which may be further eroded depending on the approach to intellectual property rights adopted by the researching organisation. It remains the case, however, that market failures — associated with positive spillovers — may still lead to levels of investment which are below the social optimum. If these spillovers are judged to be significant there may be a justification for supporting this type of research activity at regional level. Experimental development is aimed at addressing specific market opportunities or the development of specific new products or processes. This type of research may generate strong rent spillovers but is less likely to lead to very significant pure knowledge spillovers. The weakness of pure knowledge spillovers stems from (a) the extent to which experimental development leads to proprietary knowledge, and (b) the specificity of the research undertaken to the firm's own product range. Market failure-type arguments for public support of this type of R&D are therefore weakest. Within any LFR, the extent of any rent spillovers (primarily through supply chain links or research networks) will depend crucially on the extent of local linkages.

The benefits arising from an R&D centre depend, not only on the type of R&D being conducted, but also on the institutional and organisational setting of the R&D centre. For example, Blind and Grupp (1999) draw a different distinction between R&D performing organisations focussing on the generation of private and public knowledge:

> Private knowledge comes primarily from the enterprises
> themselves, but also from associations of enterprises and
> scientific and professional organisations. Public knowl-
> edge is drawn from institutions which conduct scientific
> and technical R&D. In this category are mainly universi-
> ties but also other public and semi-public research insti-
> tutions and transfer bureaux (Blind and Grupp, 1999, p.
> 452).

Centres outside universities, for example, may be more flexible
than those in a university setting due to the lack of normal academic restrictions (e.g. teaching, academic promotion criteria,
contractual restrictions etc.). Blind and Grupp (1999) suggest
that this type of restriction may shape the orientation of university-based research centres making it more difficult for them to
respond to the specific needs of their local region. Instead,
Blind and Grupp argue that university-based centres are more
likely to have a more general (i.e. national or international) orientation towards the needs of a specific sector or industry. Larger research organisations may find it difficult to relate
effectively to local small businesses, while smaller units may be
more flexible and able to adopt a more specific focus. This is
the implication drawn from their German study by Blind and
Grupp (1999) who comment that

> polytechnics tend to support small companies in their
> region, while universities and research labs transfer
> knowledge more effectively to larger companies with no
> regional priority (Blind and Grupp, 1999, p. 452).

Perhaps the other key aspect of the profile of an R&D centre is
its industrial focus. For example, some sectors may provide advances in "general purpose technologies" which may be more
useful in producing generalised productivity advances across a
range of sectors than R&D conducted in other more specific
technological areas (Trajtenberg and Bresnahan, 1995). Ten Raa
and Wolff (2000), for example, in their study of US total factor
productivity (TFP) growth, examine both within-sector and be-
tween-sector sources of productivity growth. They identify 10
sectors or "engines of growth" which made the largest contribu-

tions to TFP growth over the 1958-97 period. All of these sectors are in manufacturing with the largest sectoral TFP contributions coming from computer and office equipment and electronic components. These sectors also had the strongest spill-over effects of any manufacturing sector, although spillovers from some non-manufacturing sectors (trade, restaurants and transportation) were also important due to strong rent spillovers.[7]

Technological Landscape of the Host LFR

In addition to the characteristics of the R&D centre itself, the extent of any localised benefits will also depend crucially on the character of the host LFR. The industrial composition and absorptive capability of local firms, the strength of local knowledge dissemination networks and the integration of public and private knowledge mediating institutions will all be important as will the extent to which the R&D centre is embedded in the local economy.

One potentially useful framework within which the landscape of a host region might be considered is the regional innovation system or RIS (Braczyk et al., 1998; EU, 1998; Nasierowski and Arcelus, 1999).[8] This perspective recognises both the complexity of the innovation process, its dependence on organisational capabilities, "untraded interdependencies" (Dosi, 1988), knowledge "spillovers" (Audretsch and Feldman, 1996), knowledge integration through "open systems architecture" (Best, 2000), and the potentially important influence of

---

[7] Both effects reflect the strong forward linkages of these sectors, i.e. productivity gains or cost reductions in either sector have significant knock-on effects throughout the economy.

[8] To quote Metcalfe (1997, pp. 461-462), a national or regional system of innovation is "that set of distinct institutions which jointly and individually contribute to the development and diffusion of new technologies and which provides the framework within which governments form and implement policies to influence the innovation process. As such it is a system of interconnected institutions to create, store and transfer the knowledge, skills and artefacts which define new technology. The element of nationality follows not only from the domain of technology policy but from elements of shared language and culture which bind the system together, and from the national focus of other policies laws and regulations which condition the innovative environment."

regional innovation policy (EU, 1998). In this framework the absorptive capacity of the RIS will depend first, on the capabilities of firms and other organisations within the RIS and secondly the degree of "association" between the various elements of the RIS (e.g. the extent of any links between firms and universities etc.).

In terms of the absorptive capacity of firms, Young and Lan (1997) distinguish between the technical capability of firms and their willingness to take on board new knowledge or technology. Both aspects of firms' capabilities may be less well developed among smaller firms, which are generally less advanced in terms of use of new technologies and have lower levels of innovative capability (e.g. Roper and Anderson, 2000). In terms of technology intermediaries, Heidenreich and Krauss (1998), for example, document the positive role of "intermediate" institutions in the Baden-Württemberg RIS, while Walker (1993) notes the weakness of such institutions in the UK. Intermediate institutions may be particularly important in linking small firms with the knowledge generation sub-system given the generally observed difficulty in small firm-university or small firm-research centre linkages (e.g. Blind and Grupp, 1999).

The absorptive capacity of the RIS will also depend, however, on the systemic capability for knowledge diffusion between local firms and other organisations, in other words it will depend on the extent of local linkages and knowledge transfers. Notably the strength of local linkages and levels of knowledge transfer depends on the size of region with lower linkages in smaller regions (Hewitt-Dundas et al., 2002).[9] It is also notable, however, that numerous studies have suggested that small firms are less likely to have external links than larger businesses, and may therefore find it more difficult to benefit from any R&D centre (e.g. Love and Roper, 2001).

The geographical distribution of industry within an LFR may also be important due to "spatial economies" clustering and agglomeration (e.g. Dobkins, 1996). How significant such agglomeration effects are likely to be, however, remains uncertain. Evidence from the US (e.g. Audretsch and Feldman, 1996)

---

[9] See Oerlemans et al. (1998) for evidence on the positive relationship between firms' linkages and their innovative capability.

identifies significant R&D spillovers depending on the nature of agglomeration and research being conducted. European evidence is, if anything, more mixed.[10]

Synergy

The local benefits of an R&D centre will also depend on the extent of any potential synergies between the sectoral and technical focus of the R&D centre and its host region. At one extreme here is the literature on inward investment by multi-nationals into developing countries, where the technical weakness of indigenous firms, and a lack of synergy between the activities of local and incoming firms essentially stops any local spillovers. At the other end of the scale are situations where international R&D investment in a specific sector is attracted to a region to take advantage of existing clustering or agglomeration advantages (e.g. Silicon Valley, Tel Aviv) and by doing so further extends the local economies. In terms of an R&D centre, the availability of such synergies will depend both on the existence of existing clusters of activity within the region, the attractiveness of the region as a location for mobile R&D investment and on the character of any mobile R&D activity itself.

CONCLUSIONS

A substantial knowledge base now exists relating to the benefits of publicly supported private-sector R&D activity. Issues

---

[10] Shefer and Frenkel (1998) in their recent work on Northern Israel, for example, distinguish between the "metropolitan" area of Haifa, "intermediate" (i.e. suburban areas), and peripheral (i.e. rural) locations. Their results suggest — that for high-tech businesses at least — a metropolitan or urban location does have substantial advantages for product innovation. Brouwer and Kleinknecht (1996) using Dutch data also identified positive urban effects on some aspects on firms' innovative activity, while Harris and Trainor (1995) found that firms in urban locations in Northern Ireland were more likely to introduce new products than those elsewhere. While these studies provide a clear indication of the potential, contrary evidence suggesting the weakness of any urban or metropolitan effects is presented by Develaar and Nijkamp (1989, 1992) and Kleinknecht and Poot (1992) for the Netherlands, Koschatzky et al., (1998) for Germany, Roper (2001) for Ireland.

such as additionality, displacement and crowding-out remain important but on balance the evidence seems to support the contention that public support can lever additional, and potentially valuable, R&D activity (e.g. Griliches, 1995). This is generally important because of the positive benefits of R&D activity for firms, but more specifically important for LFRs as they try to identify effective policies to stimulate economic development and re-generation. The evidence also suggests, however, that different types of R&D activity undertaken by different types of organisations will have very different private and social benefits. For the authorities in an LFR considering R&D support, this raises an important strategic question: How, *ex ante*, can they evaluate the likely local benefits of supporting any specific R&D centre?

The approach outlined here is based around an inventory of potential global benefits (i.e. Table 6.1), and an assessment of the factors, which determine the share of any global benefits which will accrue to the LFR. This in turn depends on the nature of the R&D centre itself and the economic and institutional landscape of the LFR. For example, to what extent will there be any "rent" spillovers from the R&D centre to other firms in an LFR in terms of cost savings or quality improvements in their inputs? The evidence suggests that this will depend primarily on the strength of the downstream linkages between the firm conducting the R&D and other local companies. In larger regions this type of effect may be more significant, but Hewitt-Dundas et al. (2002) and other previous studies have suggested that local supply linkages in smaller LFRs are in general relatively weak. Similarly, to what extent will there be any "pure" knowledge spillovers from an R&D project to other local firms or organisations in an LFR? Again the evidence reviewed earlier suggests that this will depend on the type of R&D being conducted, the extent of any synergy with other production activities being undertaken in the LFR and the absorptive capacity of the LFR's regional innovation system. Near-market R&D in particular is generally thought to generate fewer "pure" knowledge spillovers than pre-competitive research activity and R&D undertaken in stand-alone enterprises is less likely to generate knowledge spillovers than that in more strongly clustered businesses. Another possible channel through which R&D might influence the wider region are the type of education and training benefits highlighted by Griliches (1995) or have positive effects on the local RIS in terms of increasing local capabilities to absorb knowledge generated elsewhere? This depends on transfers of individuals between firms, the extent of interaction between the university and industrial sectors and potential synergies between companies in terms of alternative applications of research expertise. Both are generally thought to be weaker in LFRs than in other "core" regions.

The implication is that it may be difficult for LFRs to appropriate many of the spillover benefits (both rent and pure) from R&D activity. Localised spillovers from basic research and applied research in particular may be difficult to capture locally, especially where the R&D being conducted is of limited relevance to local firms. Experimental development activity may have stronger direct benefits for the host region but even here R&D within multi-national groups may lead to the main production benefits being enjoyed elsewhere. Labour market spinoffs, as envisaged by Griliches (1995), may be more strongly localised although evidence on the scale of any such impacts remains elusive.

This is not of course to say that supporting R&D is necessarily a bad public investment in LFRs. Regional attractiveness may be enhanced by the presence of R&D centres, and these may contribute to cluster and industrial development. Moreover, the presence of R&D facilities within inward investment plants has been shown by Ruane and Kearns (2001) to enhance plant longevity. What is necessary, however, is a realisation of the potential weakness of both rent and knowledge based spillovers from R&D centres in LFRs and a structured approach to the *ex ante* evaluation of such public R&D investments.

References

Acs, Z.J., Audretsch, D.B. and Feldman, M.P. (1992), "Real effects of academic research: comment", *American Economic Review*, Vol. 82, 363-367.

Acs, Z.J., Audretsch, D.B. and Feldman, M.P. (1994), "R&D spillovers and recipient firm size" *Review of Economics and Statistics*, Vol. 76, 336-340.

Anselin, L., Varga, A. and Acs, Z.J. (2000), "Geographical spillovers and university research: A spatial econometric perspective", *Growth and Change,* Vol. 31, 501-515.

Arrow, K. (1962), "The Economic Implications of Learning by Doing", *Review of Economic Studies,* Vol. 29, No. 2, 155-173.

Audretsch, D. B. (1998), "Agglomeration and the location of innovative activity", *Oxford Review of Economic Policy*, Vol. 14, No. 2, 18-29.

Audretsch, D.B. and Feldman, M.P. (1996), "R&D spillovers and the geography of innovation and production", *American Economic Review*, Vol. 86, 630-640.

Best, M. (2000), *The Capabilities and Innovation Perspective: The Way Ahead in Northern Ireland.* Research Monograph 8, December. Belfast: Northern Ireland Economic Council.

Beugelsdijck, S. and Cornet, M. (2001), "How far do they reach? The localisation of industrial and academic spillovers in the Netherlands", Center discussion paper 2001-47.

Blind, K. and Grupp, H. (1999), "Interdependencies Between the Science and Technology Infrastructure and Innovation Activities in German Regions: Empirical Findings and Policy Consequences", *Research Policy*, Vol. 28, No. 5, 451-468.

Braczyk, H-J, Cooke, P. and Heidenreich, M. (1998), *"Regional Innovation Systems"*, London: UCL Press.

Breschi, S. and Lissoni, F. (2001), "Knowledge spillovers and local innovation systems: A critical survey", *Industrial and Corporate Change*, Vol. 10, 975-1005.

Brouwer, E. and Kleinknecht, A. (1996), "Firm size, small business presence and sales of innovative products: A micro-econometric analysis", *Small Business Economics*, Vol. 8, No. 3, 189-202.

Buxton, M. and Hanney, S. (1994) "Assessing Payback from Department of Heath Research and Development: Preliminary Report: Main Report", Research Report No 19, HERG, Brunel University.

Buxton, M. and Hanney, S. (1996), "How can Payback from Health Services Research be Assessed?", *Journal of Health Services Research and Policy,* Vol. 1, 35-43.

Buxton, M. and Hanney, S. (1997), "Assessing Payback from Department of Health Research and Development: Second Report: Main Report", Research Report 24, HERG, Brunel University.

Cohen, W.M. and Levin, R.C. (1989), "Empirical studies of innovation and market structure" in the *Handbook of Industrial Organization – Volume II,* Amsterdam: Elsevier Science Publishers.

Cooke, P., Roper, S. and Wylie, P. (2002), "Developing A Regional Innovation Strategy For Northern Ireland", Northern Ireland Economic Council, Belfast.

Crone, M. and Roper, S. (2000), "Local Learning from Multinational Plants: Knowledge Transfers in the Supply Chain", *Regional Studies,* forthcoming.

Dasgupta, P. and David, P.A. (1994), "Towards a New Economics of Science", *Research Policy,* Vol. 23, 499-514.

Develaar E. and Nijkamp, P. (1989), "Spatial Dispersion of Technological Innovation: A Case Study for the Netherlands By Means of Partial Least Squares", *Journal of Regional Science,* Vol. 29, No. 3, 325-346.

Develaar, E. and Nijkamp, P. (1992), "Operational Models on Industrial Innovation and Spatial Development: A Case Study for the Netherlands", *Journal of Scientific and Industrial Research,* Vol. 51, 253-284.

Dobkins, L.H. (1996), "Location, innovation and trade: The role of localisation and nation-based externalities", *Regional Science and Urban Economics,* Vol. 26, No 6, 591-612.

Dosi, G. (1988), "Sources, procedures and microeconomic effects of innovation", *Journal of Economic Literature,* Vol. XXVI, No. 3, 1120-1171.

Eaton, J. and Kortum, S. (1996), "Trade in ideas. Patenting and productivity in the OECD", *Journal of International Economics,* Vol. 40, No. 3-4, 251-278.

EU (1998), *Regional Innovation systems: Designing for the Future – REGIS.* Final report of the REGIS project, Targeted Socio-Economic Research (TSER) Programme (co-ordinator: Cooke, P.) European Commission DG XII.

Fernandez, E., Junquera, B. and Vazquez, C.J. (1996), "Government Support for R&D: The Spanish Case", *Technovation,* Vol. 16, No. 2, 59-66.

Griliches, Z. (1979), "Issues in assessing the contribution of research and development to productivity growth", *Bell Journal of Economics*, Vol. 10, 92-116.

Griliches, Z. (1991), "The Search for R&D Spillovers", *National Bureau for Economic Research Working Paper* No. 3768.

Griliches, Z. (1992), "The Search for R&D Spillovers", *Scandinavian Journal of Economics*, Vol. 94 (supplement), 29-47.

Griliches, Z. (1995), "R&D and Productivity: Econometric Results and Measurement Issues", in Stoneman, P. (ed.) *"Handbook of the Economics of Innovation and Technological Change"*, Oxford: Blackwell, pp. 52-89.

Guellec, D. and van Pottlesberghe de la Potterie (2001), "The Effectiveness of Public R&D Policies in OECD Countries", Paris: OECD.

Hanney, S., Packwood, T. and Buxton, M. (2000), "Evaluating the Benefits from Health Research and Development Centre Categorisation, A Model and Examples of Application", *Evaluation*, Vol. 6, No. 2, 137-160.

Harris, R.I.D. and Trainor, M. (1995), "Innovations and R&D in Northern Ireland manufacturing: A Schumpeterian approach", *Regional Studies*, Vol. 29, 593-604.

Heidenreich, M. and Krauss, G. (1998), "The Baden-Wurttemberg Production and Innovation Regime: Past Successes and New Challenges", In Braczyk, H-J, Cooke, P. and Heidenreich, M. (eds) *Regional Innovation Systems*, London: UCL Press, 214-244.

Hewitt-Dundas, N., Anderosso-Callaghan, B., Crone, M., Murray, J. and Roper, S. (2002), "Learning from the Best: Knowledge Transfers from Multinational Plants in Ireland — A North-South Comparison", NIERC/EAC.

Jaffe, A.B. (1989), "Real effects of academic research" *American Economic Review*, Vol. 79, 957-870.

Jaffe, A.B., Trajtenberg, M. and Henderson, R. (1993), "Geographic localisation of knowledge spillovers as evidenced by patent citations", *Quarterly Journal of Economics*, Vol. 108, 577-598.

Kleinknecht, A. and Poot, T.P. (1992), "Do Regions Matter for R&D?", *Regional Studies*, Vol. 32, 221-32.

Koschatzky, K., Frenkel, A, Walter, G.H. and Shefer, D. (1998), "Regional Concentration and Dynamics of Fast Growing Industries in Baden-Wurttemberg and Israel", *ISI-Arbeitspapiere Regionalforschung*, Nr 14, Institut Systemtechnik and Innovationsforschung, Karlsuhe.

Love, J.H. and Roper, S. (2001), "Location and Network Effects on Innovation Success: Evidence for UK, German and Irish Manufacturing Plants", *Research Policy*, Vol. 30, forthcoming.

Malecki, E.J. (1981), "Government-Funded R&D: Some Regional Economic Implications", *Professional Geographer*, Vol. 33, No. 1, 72-82.

Metcalfe, S. (1997), "Technology Systems and Technology Policy in an Evolutionary Framework", In *Technology, Globalisation and Economic Performance*, Archibugi, D. and Michie, J. (eds.), Cambridge University Press, pp. 286-296.

Miotti, L., Perrin, S., Sachwald, F. (2001), "Multinationales émergentes: un modèle Coréen?", *Économie internationale*, Vol. 85, No. 1, 37-62.

Nadiri, W.I. (1980), "Contributions and Determinants of R&D Expenditures in the US Manufacturing Industries", In Von Furstenberg, G. (ed.) *Capital, Efficiency and Growth,* Cambridge: Ballinger Publishing Company, pp. 361-392.

Nadiri, W.I. (1993), "Innovations and Technological Spillovers", *National Bureau for Economic Research Working Paper*, No. 4423.

Nasierowski, W. and Arcelus, F.J. (1999), "Inter-relationships among the Elements of National Innovation Systems: A Statistical Evaluation", *European Journal of Operations Research*, Vol. 119, No. 2, 235-253.

Nelson, R.R. (1959), "The Simple Economics of Basic Scientific Research", *Journal of Political Economy*, Vol. 67, 27-43.

Oerlemans, L.A.G., Meus, M.T.H. and Boekema, F.W.M. (1998), "Do Networks Matter for Innovation? The Usefulness of the Economic Network Approach in Analysing Innovation", *Tijdschrift voor Economische en Sociale Geografie*, Vol. 89, No. 3, 298-309.

Piergiovanni, R. and Santarelli, E. (2001), "Patents and the geographic localisation of R&D spillovers in French manufacturing" *Regional Studies*, Vol. 35, 697-702.

Reddy, P. (1997), "New trends in globalisation of corporate R&D and implications for innovation capability in host countries: A survey from India", *World Development*, Vol. 25, No. 11, 1821-1838.

Romer, P. (1990), "Endogenous Technological Change", *Journal of Political Economy,* Vol. 98, s71-s102.

Roper, S. (2001), "Innovation, Networks and Plant Location: Evidence for Ireland", *Regional Studies*, Vol. 35, No. 3, 215-228.

Roper, S. and Anderson, J. (2000), *"Innovation and E-Commerce: A Cross-Border Comparison of Irish Manufacturing Plants"*, Belfast: NIERC, Research Report 17.

Roper, S. and Frenkel, A. (2000), "Different paths to Success – The growth of the Electronics Sector in Ireland and Israel", *Environment and Planning C*, Vol. 18, No. 6, 651-666.

Roper, S. and Hewitt-Dundas, N. (1998), *Innovation, Networks and the Diffusion of Manufacturing Best Practice: A Comparison of Northern Ireland and the Republic of Ireland*, Belfast: NIERC.

Roper, S. and Love, J.H. (2001), "The Determinants of Export Performance: Panel Data Evidence for Irish Manufacturing Plants", *NIERC, Working Paper* No 67, Belfast.

Ruane, F. and Kearns, A. (2001), "The tangible contribution of R&D-spending foreign-owned plants to a host region: A plant level study of the Irish manufacturing sector (1980-1996)", *Research Policy*, Vol. 30, No. 2, 227-244.

Shefer, D. and Frenkel, A. (1998), "Local Milieu and Innovations: Some Empirical Results", *Annals of Regional Science*, Vol. 32, 185-200.

Smith, K. (1989), "Public Support for Civil R&D in the UK: Limitations of Recent Policy Debate", *Research Policy*, Vol. 18, 99-109.

Ten Raa, T. and Wolff, E.N. (2000), "Engines of Growth in the US Economy", *Structural Change and Economic Dynamics*, Vol. 11, No. 4, 473-489.

Trajtenberg, M. and Bresnahan, T.F. (1995), "General Purpose Technologies — Engines Of Growth", *Journal of Econometrics*, Vol. 65, No. 1, 83-108.

Turok, I. (1993), "Inward investment and local linkages: How deeply embedded is "silicon glen"?", *Regional Studies*, Vol. 27, No. 5, 401-417.

Veugelers, R. and Cassiman, B. (1999), "Make and Buy in Innovation Strategies: Evidence from Belgian Manufacturing Firms", *Research Policy*, Vol. 28, 63-80.

Walker, W. (1993), "National Innovation Systems: Britain", In Nelson, R R (ed) *National Innovation Systems: A Comparative Analysis*, Oxford: OUP, pp. 158-191.

Young, S. and Lan, P. (1997), "Technology transfer to China through foreign direct Investment", *Regional Studies*, Vol. 31, 669-680.

Zucker, L.G., Darby, M.R. and Armstrong, J. (1998a), "Geographically localised knowledge: Spillovers or markets?", *Economic Inquiry*, Vol. 36, 65-86.

Zucker, L.G., Darby, M.R. and Brewer, M.B. (1998b), "Intellectual human capital and the birth of US biotechnology enterprises", *American Economic Review*, Vol. 88, 290-306.

Chapter 7

THE SPATIAL DISTRIBUTION OF KNOWLEDGE CREATION CAPABILITY IN IRISH REGIONS

Bernadette Andreosso-O'Callaghan, Nola Hewitt-Dundas, John Murray and *Stephen Roper*

INTRODUCTION

The progress in economic growth theory in recent decades has facilitated the understanding of the variables impinging on the growth process across and within countries. The "new" growth theory purports to explain the wealth disparities across and within countries with due reference to the spatially unbalanced access to knowledge and innovation capability (see Morgenroth in Chapter 5 of this volume). In the light of the wealth disparities observed across counties and broad regions in Ireland — to such an extent that some counties became amalgamated into a new region keeping thereby their "objective 1" status, and splitting for the first time and officially the country into two broad NUTS 2[1] regions — the question of knowledge and innovation regional disparities becomes pertinent.

---

[1] The NUTS (Nomenclature des Unités Territoriales Statistiques) specifies four different levels of regional disaggregation (0-4), with NUTS 0 being the member state. Most analyses of regional imbalance are conducted at the NUTS 2 level.

The primary objective of this chapter is therefore to provide some understanding of the geographical distribution of knowledge creation capability in Ireland. Knowledge creation capability is defined on the basis of R&D intensity and of knowledge transfer flows. A few intriguing questions are addressed such as: is there a clear correspondence between the dispersion of knowledge creation capability and the dispersion of wealth in Ireland? Conversely, is there evidence of "learning regions" or innovative *milieux* in the poorer part of the country?

After a brief review of the theoretical background underpinning the study, we then examine regional disparities in Ireland using both macroeconomic and innovation-based variables in the next two sections. The analysis of regional disparities in the next section is based on a fine partitioning of the Irish economic space so as to determine whether the distribution of knowledge creation capability is more uneven within as opposed to between regions. Conclusive avenues will be proffered in a final section.

THEORETICAL FOUNDATIONS FOR THE STUDY

Our work is centred around the linking filament that connects knowledge, space and growth. It highlights the knowledge potential that a region possesses in order to grow. This approach is best understood as being enshrined in the so-called "new" growth models. Indeed, the field of regional economics has not escaped from the authoritative prominence of endogenous growth models, which were developed in the 1980s by Romer (1986) and Lucas (1985). Highlighting the importance of knowledge accumulation to economic growth, integrating increasing returns to scale and imperfect competition in dynamic general equilibrium frameworks, the new growth theory is now well established in the field of regional economics.[2] Endogenous growth models and their theoretical developments have been used to explain regional growth in the European Union (Cheshire and Magrini, 2000), in the US (Ceh, 2001; Rupasingha et al.,

---

[2] Poot and Nijkamp (1998) provide a survey of studies applying the new growth models to regional economic perspectives.

2002), as well as in Asian countries (Park, 2000). Ceh (2001) singles out skilled labour as being an important stimulus to regional technology production in the USA, whereas Rupasingha et al. (2002) formulate a county-level growth model that links income growth to a set of social and institutional dimensions, such as ethnicity. Park (2000) discusses the impact of globalisation and of information and communication technology on the reconfiguration of the Pacific Rim's economic space. The author highlights in particular the parallel development of economically integrated regions and of city regions in the Pacific Rim in recent decades. Adapting an endogenous growth framework to the analysis of growth determinants in 122 EU regions, Cheshire and Magrini (2000) develop a new model centred on the concept of "tacit knowledge". This refers to the non-written personal heritage of individuals or groups, a feature which is spatially concentrated.

Whether growth remains spatially confined (with the well-known self-reinforcing effects through time) or, on the contrary diffuses to adjacent regions, is still largely open to debate. Indeed, the main theoretical basis that illustrates the relationship between knowledge and space (or innovation and space) can be grouped into two broad strands:

- **The Urban-Hierarchy Model.** According to this strand of analysis, metropolitan areas can benefit from specific agglomeration advantages, such as a critical mass in a specific field of research, and are therefore more likely to be knowledge driven and to innovate. This view highlights the fact that innovation activity and high-tech firms are not evenly distributed spatially. Borrowing from other theoretical strands such as the product cycle model, this model advocates that because of the existence of agglomeration advantages, e.g. knowledge externalities, it is best for knowledge and innovative capability such as R&D to be concentrated spatially, so as to allow the maximisation of these externalities. In the long-term, divergence could be self-reinforcing, as was expounded by Verdoorn's law according to which regions with higher growth rates of productivity experience also higher growth rates of output (Verdoorn, 1949). However, in the best of all cases, and thanks to information flows and other possible interactions, spillovers to neighbouring regions could eventually take place.[3]

- **The Learning Region.** On the other hand, another strand of the literature has emerged in the 1980s, which started to emphasise the existence of specific regional agglomeration economies, i.e. lying outside the urban centres. These regions may certainly not benefit from all the agglomeration economies observed in the classical urban centres (for example, their population may be more dispersed spatially), yet they are able to grow. These specific sub-national growth enclaves are referred to indiscriminately as "innovative *milieux*", "local systems of innovation", or "learning regions".[4] They are best evidenced by the high-tech clusters in the US, the industrial districts in the third Italy (Sforzi, 1990), and by the existence of technopoles and technological enclaves either in special economic zones throughout the world, or elsewhere (Castells and Hall, 1994).[5] Of extreme importance in these "innovative *milieux*" are the specific agglomeration effects that are explained by the sociological and cultural forces underlying the "network effects". These can simply be defined as inter-firm relations, and also as the proximity existing between research centres and the firms in a given region. The network effects are seen as an essential feature of the dynamics of the regional growth process in the literature on local economic development. In the words of Breschi and Lissoni (2001, p. 270),

---

[3] This is close, for example, to Caniels and Verspagen's model according to which inter-regional knowledge spillovers determine the growth of regions (2001).

[4] For a review of the literature on these sub-national innovation enclaves, see Andreosso-O'Callaghan (2001).

[5] On the emergence of successful non-metropolitan areas in Northern Italy, and on the factors (of which information flows) explaining such success, see Camagni and Capello (1990). On a comparison between the development of high-tech centres in France and in the UK, see Druilhe and Garnsey (2000). With regard to the emergence of technopoles and science parks, etc., in Asian countries, see for example Shin (2001) for the specific case of South Korea.

"knowledge flows are an extremely important agglomeration force, and [...] a very large part of these flows take place at the local and regional level". This is a vision close to that of Cheshire and Magrini's (2000) and also to Park's, according to whom "networking [such as inter-firm relations] is a primary condition for the formation of territory-based innovation systems" (Park, 2000, p. 337). Network effects, the intensity of which is determined by socio-cultural factors, are judged important for the process of knowledge transfer and innovation.

Another explanation for the emergence of growth regions is the presence of decreasing returns in congested and richer regions, implying that physical investment and innovative investment in core areas become less and less efficient, justifying thereby their relocation in the periphery. This in turn is a means to revive the lagging regions. However, the existence of decreasing returns in congested and metropolitan areas is only one among many explanations for the revival of laggard regions throughout the world. Active regional policies have stimulated R&D and innovation capability in many lagging regions of the world. The case of the EU provides probably one of the most pertinent examples of how the innovation-led regional policy has been enthused as one of the main driving forces behind regional development in recent years. The ultimate objective of the recently developed EU Regional Innovation Strategy (RIS) is to keep talent and to stimulate growth, allowing thereby lagging regions to catch-up with the wealthy core. According to Rodriguez-Pose (2000), investing in R&D in the poorer regions of the EU is probably the only viable solution to prevent the increase in the technology and knowledge gap between core and periphery.

Work on the spatial distribution of innovative activities has primarily concerned the large economies of the world.[6] Studies pertaining to small open economies such as Ireland are much more rare. The notable exceptions to this trend are the few contributions done on the innovation capability of regions in Israel

---

[6] See, for example, the recent contribution by Bade and Nerlinger (2000) on the spatial distribution of new-technology-based firms in the case of Germany.

by Shefer and Frankel (1998) and the work done on Scandinavian countries. For example, Kangasharju (2000) estimates the effects of the regional factors on firm formation in Finland, and finds that the average size of firms is an important and critical factor. Turning to Ireland, very few studies have attempted to analyse the growth and innovation processes by partitioning the country into its sub-regional components. It is only in the last few years that a few publications have appeared in this area. For example, McCartney and Teague (1997) investigate the spatial dispersion of innovation in the area of human resource management in Ireland. Roper (2001) analyses the importance of locational factors on the firms' innovative activities throughout the country and finds no evidence that agglomeration economies represent any specific environment to plants in terms of their probability to innovate. Finally, Andreosso-O'Callaghan (2001) shows that in the mid-1990s, the Shannon region combined all the features of what describes best a local system of innovation.

REGIONAL DISPARITIES IN THE REPUBLIC OF IRELAND

The importance of the regional divide in Ireland has been the subject of a rich debate since the initiation of the export-led growth policy in the late 1950s. To combat the unbalanced growth process, a number of local initiatives were deployed throughout the years, although this was done in a rather erratic way, and with little continuity. The 1950s and 1960s were a period of active regional policy in Ireland. In particular, the 1950s saw the establishment of the Shannon Free Zone, the first free trade zone of modern times, and the Lichfield Report (Lichfield and Associates 1967) on the Mid-West Region enabled the setting-up of the first technopole in the Mid-West region of the country. From the mid-1970s to the late 1980s, little was done in terms of promoting the regional or local dimension of development in Ireland, for the emphasis at the time was on macro-economic issues such as the high debt to GDP ratio and high inflation rates. The regional debate was revived towards the end of the 1980s, and it culminated recently with the geographical partitioning of the country into two NUTS-2 regions.[7] During this second period of active regional policy, some institutions were created at local level (such as the County Enterprise Boards), and other local development initiatives were initiated such as the Area-Based Partnerships (Shortall, 1994; OECD, 1996), the EU-initiated LEADER and RIS programmes,[8] and the Irish Community Support Framework (Fitzpatrick and Associates, 1997).

As a result, and partly thanks to the implementation of these different initiatives, living standards across Irish regions diverged only slightly during the period of economic downturn, i.e. between 1979 and 1996 (O'Leary, 2001).[9] The many efforts done during the 1980s and 1990s in terms of promoting local development initiatives, and of rejuvenating some laggard regions did help to lessen the importance of the regional divide in Ireland. An intriguing phenomenon is that although Ireland now has two distinct regions (the BMW region and The South) in terms of wealth dispersion, the split between the two broad NUTS 2 regions is not clear-cut when one refers to criteria of innovation performance. Indeed, and according to recent EU figures (Eurostat, 2001), GDP per person in PPS terms in 1998 ranged from €15,000 to €20,000 in the BMW region, as against €20,000 to €25,000 in the rest of the country. This divide appears also clearly in terms of employment in both the high-tech manufacturing and service sector. Curiously, when it comes to the number of patent applications per capita, the split between the two broad regions seems to disappear. The question there-

---

[7] The seven planning regions have been grouped into the BMW region (Border, Midlands and West) and what we call in this chapter "The South". The BMW region comprises 13 counties, whereas the 14 other counties are part of the more economically advanced south.

[8] LEADER: Liaisons entre actions de développement de l'économie rurale. The RIS (Regional Innovation Strategy) programme targeted specifically the Shannon region.

[9] It should be borne in mind that the period under review in O'Leary's paper encompasses nevertheless 3 years of economic boom. Also, the period of economic retrenchment following an era of post-war continued economic growth is a phenomenon observable in most economies of the EU and of the OECD. In the case of Ireland, this phenomenon happened later.

fore becomes: is there a clear correspondence between the economic performance of Irish regions and their knowledge and innovative capability? How is knowledge creation capability distributed across Irish regions? Before tackling this issue, we will provide up-dated quantified evidence of the regional divide using macroeconomic indicators. Whenever possible, the analysis will be conducted at the level of the seven Irish sub- regions, which are: the three BMW sub-regions mentioned above, and the Greater Dublin, Mid-West, South East and South West sub-regions. Data relating to the macroeconomic performance of these seven Irish sub-regions started being collected and published in 1991. Table 7.1 gives an insight into the spatial distribution of wealth (measured by gross value added per person), population, and labour in Ireland in 1998. It also gives an indication in relation to the structural composition of production.

Table 7.1: Distribution of GVA, Employment, Population, and Manufacturing & Service Activity Across Regions (1998)

	GVA/ Capita (£) [#]	Population (000)	Labour (000)	% of GVA in Mfg. Sector [†]	% of GVA in Service Sector
BMW	10,816	979	363	36.4	54.0
Border	11,381	408	146	42.0	8.7
Midland	9,894	208	77	30.4	59.3
West	10,711	362	140	33.0	57.5
Greater Dublin*	17,426	1,457	639	33.9	65.1
Mid West	13,182	322	129	44.0	48.7
South East	11,531	397	149	42.3	47.8
South West	16,958	551	214	50.0	44.1
State	14,611	3,705	1,494	38.7	56.5

Source: CSO Regional accounts, Dublin, various years.

(*) Dublin plus Mid East

(#) At Basic prices. These figures are now harmonised to comply with the EU system of accounts (ESA).

(†) These figures include also the gross value added of the building and construction industries.

In the BMW broad region, wealth per capita, measured on the basis of gross value added figures, is only 74 per cent that of the average for the country, and less than two-thirds that of the greater Dublin sub-region. When taking the "Midland" sub-region as a unit of reference, the gap is even greater. This is also a region characterised by slightly lower labour participation rates. With 26 per cent of the total population, the BMW region accounts for only 24 per cent of total labour in the country. However, combining this small gap with large differences in terms of GVA implies that labour productivity rates are lower in the BMW region.

USING INNOVATION-RELATED INDICATORS FOR THE ANALYSIS OF SPATIAL DISPARITIES

The BMW' s share of high-tech manufacturing employment and output, compared with that of the wealthiest region of the country can easily be computed from the Central Statistics Office (CSO) data providing a geographical breakdown of manufacturing activity in Ireland. Based on the Eurostat (2001) definition, a high-tech industry is defined on the basis of its direct as well as *indirect* R&D intensity. This is an industry characterised by a high R&D expenditure/Value Added ratio, as well as by a high R&D content in the inputs used. The CSO nomenclature of manufacturing activity by region is unfortunately based only on a two-digit level. Consequently, the pharmaceutical industry, which is the high-tech component *par excellence* of the Chemicals sector, cannot be singled out in our analysis. For our purpose, we have classified the following industries in the high-tech sector: Chemicals (24), Machinery and Equipment (39), Electrical and Optical Equipment (30-33), and Transport Equipment (34-35). The use of location quotients helps determine the degree of spatial concentration of high-tech activities (Table 7.2). We have computed these location quotients on the basis of both employment and productivity variables, defined as the average net output per person engaged in high-tech industries. For the employment variable, LQ_N is defined as:

$$LQ_N = \frac{N_r^{HT} \Big/ N_{IRL}^{HT}}{N_r^T \Big/ N_{IRL}^T}$$

where: N_r^{HT} is the manufacturing employment in the four high-tech sectors in region r; N_{IRL}^{HT} is the manufacturing employment in the 4 high-tech sectors in Ireland as a whole; N_r^T refers to the total manufacturing employment in region r, and, N_{IRL}^T is total manufacturing employment in Ireland.

Table 7.2: Spatial Differences in terms of High-Tech Employment and Productivity (1999)

	High-Tech Employment	Productivity
BMW	0.95	0.95
South	1.04	1.01

Source: CSO (2001) Regional Accounts, CSO: Dublin.

As can be seen in Table 7.2, high-tech employment is almost evenly distributed across the two regions, *i.e.* the share of the BMW region in total high-tech employment is not that different from its share in total manufacturing employment, producing a LQ_N ratio of 0.95. Also, a small regional dichotomy between the more advanced East, South and Mid-West region and the BMW region appears at the level of productivity performance. However, it should be noted that in the BMW region, the average productivity ratio in high-tech industries is only a third that of the southern part of the country, whereas average productivity in the total manufacturing sector of the BMW region is half that of the South. Although the LQ indicators lessen regional differences between regions (given that it relates the performance of a region to that of the country as a whole), when compared together, the two broad Irish regions display an important high-tech productivity gap. What divides the two regions is less their employment patterns or their high-tech activities *per se*, than the quality of this employment and of these activities. A wide productivity gap between the two regions reflects indeed wide differentials in terms of high-tech plants quality as well as jobs quality in these plants.

According to the CSO data (CSO, 2001), foreign-owned plants in these high-tech sectors represent the major bulk of employment and of output. For example, foreign-owned plants in the BMW region accounted in 1999 for 90 per cent of gross output in the Chemicals sector (24); 67 per cent in the Machinery and Equipment sector (29); and more than 94 per cent in Electrical and Optical Equipment (30-33).[10] Multi-national Enterprise (MNE) plants in Ireland are therefore predominantly of a high-tech type, and are at the forefront of technological change both in terms of knowledge capability (i.e. R&D intensity), and of product and process innovation. Bearing these considerations in mind, we can now turn to an analysis of more refined innovation-related indicators using data gathered with the help of a survey conducted in 2000. These data were collected with the help of face-to-face interviews with senior managers of large (i.e. with more than 200 employees) foreign-owned MNE plants in Ireland.[11] Based on a semi-structured questionnaire, interviews involved 61 plants (46 per cent of the target group). The relatively high response rate and the lack of any statistically significant difference between the ownership and industrial composition of the target group and our sample means that results are likely to be representative.

Out of the 388 variables contained in the data set, we isolate those specifically related to knowledge creation capability in a regional context. As the MNE plants in Ireland are viewed as a reservoir of knowledge that eventually spills over to local and indigenous firms, the emphasis is therefore placed here on two major variables: the R&D intensity of MNE plants, and the intensity of knowledge transfers. Although difficult to quantify, the intensity of R&D and of knowledge transfers implies the selec-

---

[10] Note that this ratio is only 28 per cent in the case of Transport Equipment (34-35). Output and employment in this sector represent however a very small fraction of total output and employment in the 4 high-tech sectors. This is also the sector with the lowest productivity rates.

[11] A plant is said to belong to a foreign-owned MNE if its parent company own manufacturing plants in more than one country.

tion of appropriate indicators. Because of the reluctance (or perhaps inability) of many interviewed firms to release precise quantified information in relation to their R&D expenditure, R&D intensity is defined on the basis of whether a plant conducts research, and whether it possesses an R&D department. Knowledge transfers refer to information flows generated by MNE plants and received by their indigenous suppliers. There are however two broad types of indicators which help measure the intensity of knowledge transfers. One type is related to normal trading relations, and refers to knowledge transferred via routine business relationships. These encompass the feedback on supplier performance and the contacts to discuss technical issues related to the inputs supplied. Both feedback and contacts can be assessed on a weekly, monthly or quarterly basis. The other type of indicators refers to more developmental MNE-supplier business interactions. These are:

- Collaboration between the supplier and the MNE plant on new product development

- Assistance provided by the MNE plant to the supplier company to help with the implementation of quality control or assurance systems,

- Provision of information to the supplier company by the MNE plant relating to other business opportunities within the wider group, and

- Auditing of suppliers' manufacturing operations by staff from the MNE plant.

The rationale for highlighting the specific importance of the knowledge transfer variable is that, as emphasised in many studies such as those by both Breschi and Lissoni (2001) and Cheshire and Magrini (2000), knowledge flows are viewed as an important agglomeration force and are very likely to take place at the local level. Consequently, the knowledge creation capability of a region is best appraised with the help of quantified information on the knowledge actually flowing from innovation-driven firms (the MNE plants in our case) to all other firms (indigenous) that interact with them in the region.

Tables 7.3 and 7.4 depict the spatial distribution of R&D and knowledge transfer intensity across Irish regions during the year 2000. As can be seen, more than half of all MNE plants in the total sample claim to conduct research, and this research is mostly conducted in a research department.

Table 7.3: Regional Distribution of R&D Intensity (2000)

	Number of R&D-driven MNE Plants	Number of Plants with an R&D Department	Number of Plants Conducting Pure Research (*)	Total Number of Surveyed Plants
South-West	9	7	3	13
Dublin	8	8	3	17
Mid-West	5	5	2	7
South-East	4	3	0	8
Border	4	3	2	4
Midlands	1	0	0	1
West	7	6	5	11
BMW	12	9	7	16
South	26	23	8	45
Total	38	32	15	61

(*) Pure research on product technology.

Results of tests for independence (NUTS 2 level): Conducting R&D: χ^2= 1.490, α= 0.222; Plants with an R&D department: χ^2= 0.074, α = 0.784; Conducting pure research: χ^2= 4.293 , α = 0.038.

Source: Authors' survey.

Whereas the proportion of firms with an R&D department is roughly the same in the two broad regions, the BMW region is characterised by a much larger share of research active MNE plants than the South. Also, the plants in the laggard BMW region undertake more systematically pure research than the MNE plants in the richer south. In order to verify the significance of these results, we use the chi-square and Pearson statistic.[12]

---

[12] The chi-square is calculated with the following formula, where r and c refer to the number of rows and columns respectively: $\chi^2 = \sum_{i=1}^{r}\sum_{j=1}^{c}\frac{\left(f_{oij} - f_{eij}\right)^2}{f_{eij}}$.

Table 7.4: Regional Breakdown of Knowledge Transfer Activity (2000)

	Normal Trading Relations		Developmental Knowledge Transfer Activities			
	Monthly Contact on Technical Issues	Monthly Feedback on Performance	Collaboration on Product Development (*)	Assist with Quality Assurance Systems	Audit Suppliers' Manufacturing	Info on Other Business Opportunities
South-West	6	2	5.6	7	9	8
Dublin	4	3	4.3	14	11	12
Mid-West	1	1	3.5	2	6	4
South-East	2	1	3.6	5	7	6
Border	0	0	2.3	1	1	4
Midlands	1	0	0.6	0	0	1
West	6	3	3	4	7	8
BMW	7	3	7	5	8	13
SOUTH	13	7	16	28	33	30
TOTAL	20	10	23	33	41	43

(*): Since the type of collaboration on product development can be done at three different levels, at senior management level, middle management level or shop floor level, we have taken into account all three levels in our analysis. Consequently, the numbers in this column refer to the average number of plants who collaborate on product development issues with their supplier per region.

Results of tests for independence (NUTS 2 level): Contact on technical issues: $\chi^2= 1.606$, $\alpha = 0.205$; Feedback on performance: $\chi^2= 0.087$, $\alpha = 0.766$; Quality assurance: $\chi^2= 0.254$, $\alpha= 0.613$; Audit: $\chi^2= 1.959$, $\alpha=0.161$; Information on business opportunities elsewhere in the group: $\chi^2= 0.777$, $\alpha =0.377$.

Source: Authors' survey.

A comparison of the proportion of plants undertaking research in each broad regional category (BMW versus the South) suggests that there is no significant difference in the observed cell frequencies. In other words, being located in the BMW region or outside does not make any difference to the likelihood of conducting R&D. The same result applies to the proportion of plants in each broad region possessing an R&D department. The only variable for which the chi-square value is significant (at the 5 per cent level) is the one pertaining to the proportion of plants conducting pure research in the two broad regions. Surprisingly, the proportion of MNE plants undertaking pure research is significantly greater in the BMW region than it is in the rest of the country. As for the 6 knowledge transfer activities, the results of the tests suggest again that for all variables, the probability of transferring knowledge in one way or another in the BMW region is the same as the probability of transferring knowledge in the richer south. Indeed, the null hypothesis must be accepted for all 6 variables, given the non-significant values of the chi-square.

An explanation for these puzzling results may be the non-homogeneity of the two broad regions. It may be that the disparities within broad regions may be more important than those between NUTS 2 regions. An explanation for this could be the existence of pockets of knowledge creation capability (that is of *milieux* conducive to knowledge creation and to innovation) in the laggard region of Ireland.

BETWEEN-REGION AND WITHIN-REGION DISPARITIES IN KNOWLEDGE CREATION CAPABILITY

The analysis of between and within region disparities of a certain phenomenon is best appraised with the help of an entropy index. We can compute a simple measure for the degree to which knowledge creation capability differs spatially within and between regions. The general formulation of the entropy index is given as follows.[13]

---

[13] Theil (1967) and Theil and Friedman (1973) developed a similar index for the study of income inequality among and within regions of the world.

$$E = \sum_{i=1}^{n} S_i . \log\left(\frac{1}{S_i}\right) \tag{1}$$

where x_i can denote a region i's share of a chosen indicator. The inequality is maximum, i.e., in our case knowledge creation capability is spatially perfectly concentrated when the index is equal to 0.[14]

This entropy index presents a major attractive feature, which is that it possesses aggregation properties. In our example, by grouping the 7 sub-regions into 2 broad regions, the BMW and the South, we will be able to decompose the index into the "between-region" (E_B) and "within-region" (E_W) contribution to the total index inequality measure.

We can write: $E_T = E_W + E_B$, which implies that the total entropy index can be decomposed into its two components.

The "between-region" index is given as follows:

$$E_B = \sum_{r=1}^{n} K_r \log \frac{1}{K_r} \tag{2}$$

where K_r is the relative share of knowledge creation capability in region r (with r_1 = BMW and r_2 = South).

The "within-region" index is written as follows:

$$E_w = \sum_{r=1}^{n} K_r \sum_{i \in R} \frac{K_i}{K_r} . \log \frac{K_r}{K_i} \tag{3}$$

where K_i denotes the share of knowledge creation capability in sub-region i, with $i \in R$, and R being the number of broad regions in the country.

We use two variables for the analysis of knowledge disparities: one simply refers to the spatial distribution of R&D departments, and the other concerns a knowledge transfer indicator calculated on the basis of the 6 knowledge transfer activities shown in Table 7.4. The results are displayed in Table 7.5.

---

[14] Indeed, it is easy to see that if, for example, all R&D is concentrated in one sub-region, $S_i = 1 \Rightarrow E=0$.

Table 7.5: Entropy Index of Inequality

	E_B	E_W	E_T
Plants with an R&D department	0.2573	0.1564	0.413
Plants engaged in knowledge transfer	0.2427	0.1547	0.397

Source: Authors' calculations based on the survey.

As can be seen, there is very little difference between the results in terms of total entropy (E_T), implying that research and knowledge transfer activities are equally concentrated in Ireland. The analysis of the intensity of disparities within, as opposed to, between regions shows that in the case of both variables, concentration within broad regions is much more pronounced than concentration between these regions. This shows that each of the two NUTS 2 regions in Ireland is far from being homogenous, at least in terms of the selected innovation-based indicators. This does lend support to the fact that there are innovative *milieux* in the poor region of the country, such as the one represented by the Galway agglomeration.

CONCLUSIONS

This analysis has shown that the regional divide between the poorer BMW Irish region and the South exists in wealth terms, and also in terms of productivity in the high-tech sectors. This reflects a general uneven distribution of the quality of both high-tech plants and jobs. An interesting question is to examine whether there is a clear correspondence between these regional economic disparities and the disparities in terms of knowledge creation. Based on the data of a survey of MNE plants in Ireland, we find however that whether an MNE plant is located in the rich South rather than in the poor BMW region does not make any difference to its propensity of engaging in R&D and of transferring knowledge. There is therefore little support for the correspondence mentioned above. These puzzling results are greatly explained by the fact that the disparities in terms of knowledge creation capability are much more visible within the broad regions than between these regions. This implies that there exists, in the economically laggard region of Ireland, a number of pockets of innovative activity, of learning regions. Perhaps, these innovative *milieux* in the BMW region weaken the economic rationale for splitting the country into two broad regions for the sole purpose of implementing European regional policy tools.

References

Andreosso-O'Callaghan, B. (2001), "Territory, research and technology linkages — Is the Shannon region a propitious local system of innovation?" *Entrepreneurship & Regional Development*, Vol. 12, 69-87.

Bade, F. J. and Nerlinger, E. A (2000), "The spatial distribution of new technology-based firms: Empirical results for West-Germany". *Papers in Regional Science*, Vol. 79, No. 2, 155-76.

Breschi, S. and Lissoni, F. (2001), "Localised knowledge spillovers vs innovative milieux: Knowledge 'tacitness' reconsidered". *Papers in Regional Science,* Vol. 80, No. 3, 255-73.

Camagni, R. and Capello, R. (1990), "Towards a definition of the manoeuvring space of local development initiatives: Italian success stories of local development – theoretical conditions and practical experiences", In Walter B. Stöhr, (ed) *Global Change and Local Response — Initiatives for Economic Regeneration in Contemporary Europe.* London: Mansell, pp. 328-53.

Caniels, M.C.J and Verspagen, B. (2001), "Barriers to knowledge spillovers and regional convergence in an evolutionary model". *Journal of Evolutionary Economics*, Vol. 11, No. 3, 307-29.

Castells, M. and Hall, P. (1994), *Technopoles of the World: The Making of the Twenty-first Century Industrial Complex.* London: Routledge.

Ceh, B. (2001), "Regional innovation potential in the United States: Evidence of Spatial transformation". *Papers in Regional Science,* Vol. 80, No. 3, 297-316.

Cheshire, P. and Magrini, S. (2000), "Endogenous Processes in European Regional Growth: Convergence and Policy". *Growth and Change*, Vol. 31, No. 4, 455-79.

Central Statistics Office (CSO) (2001), *Regional Accounts.* Dublin: Central Statistics Office.

Central Statistics Office (CSO), *Regional Accounts*, Dublin: Central Statistics Office, various years.

Druilhe, C. and Garnsey, E. (2000), "Emergence and growth of high-tech activity in Cambridge and Grenoble". *Entrepreneurship and Regional Development*, Vol. 12, 163-77.

Eurostat (2001), *Region: Statistical Yearbook*. EC, Luxembourg.

Fitzpatrick and Associates (1997), *Mid-term evaluation: Regional impact of the Community Support Framework for Ireland 1994-1999*. Dublin.

Kangasharu, A. (2000), "Regional variations in firm formation: Panel and cross-section data evidence from Finland". *Papers in Regional Science,* Vol. 79, No. 4, 355-73.

Lichfield and Associates (1967), *Report and Advisory Plan for the Limerick Region,* Dublin: Stationery Office.

Lucas, R.E., Jr. (1985), "On the Mechanics of Economic Development", *Marshall Lecture,* May.

McCartney J. and Teague, P. (1997), "Workplace Innovations in the Republic of Ireland". *Economic and Social Review,* Vol. 28, No. 4, 381-399.

OECD (1996), *Ireland: Local Partnerships and Social Innovation*. (Prepared by C. Sabel and the LEED Programme; Paris).

O'Leary, E. (2001), "Convergence of Living Standards among Irish Regions: The Roles of Productivity, Profit Outflows and Demography, 1960-96". *Regional Studies,* Vol. 35, No. 3, 197-205.

Park, S.O. (2000), "Regional Issues in the Pacific Rim (A Note and Comment)". *Papers in Regional Science.* Vol. 79, No. 3, 333-42.

Poot, J. and Nijkamp, P. (1998), "Spatial perspectives on new theories of economic growth". *Annals of Regional Science,* Vol. 32, 7-38.

Rodriguez-Pose, A. (2001), "Is R&D investment in lagging areas of Europe worthwhile? Theory and empirical evidence". *Papers in Regional Science,* Vol. 80, No. 3, 275-95.

Romer, P.M. (1986), "Increasing Returns and Long-Run Growth". *Journal of Political Economy,* Vol. 94, 1002-38.

Roper, S. (2001), "Innovation, Networks and Plant Location: Some Evidence for Ireland". *Regional Studies,* Vol. 35, No. 3, 215-28.

Rupasingha, A., S.J. Goetz and D. Freshwater (2002), "Social and Institutional factors as determinants of economic growth: Evidence from the United States counties". *Papers in Regional Science,* Vol. 81, No. 2, 139-55.

Sforzi, F. (1990), "The quantitative importance of Marshallian industrial districts in the Italian Economy", In F. Pyke, G. Becattini, and W. Sengenberger, (eds), *Industrial Districts and Inter-Firm Cooperation in Italy*. Geneva: International Institute for Labour Studies, pp. 75-107.

Shefer, D. and Frenkel, A. (1998), "Local milieu and innovations: Some empirical results". *The Annals of Regional Science,* Vol. 32, No. 2, 185-200.

Shin, Dong-Ho (2001), "An alternative approach to developing science parks: A case study from Korea". *Papers in Regional Science,* Vol. 80, No. 1, 103-11.

Shortall, S. (1994), "The Irish Rural Development Paradigm — An Exploratory Analysis". *Economic and Social Review*, Vol. 25, 233-60.

Theil, H. (1967), *Economics and Information Theory.* New York: American Elsevier Publishing Company, and Amsterdam: North-Holland Publishing Company.

Theil, H. and Friedman, Y. (1973), "Regional Per Capita Incomes and Income Inequalities: Point Estimates and Their Standard Errors". *Journal of the American Statistical Association,* Vol. 68, No. 343, 531-39.

Verdoorn, P.J. (1949), *Fattori che regolano lo sviluppo della produttività del lavoro*, L'industria.

Chapter 8

ORGANISATIONAL CAPABILITIES AND ENVIRONMENTAL REGULATION: THE CASE OF THE PHARMACEUTICAL SECTOR IN IRISH REGIONS

Rachel Hilliard and David Jacobson[1]

INTRODUCTION

This chapter develops a broader than conventional understanding of regional policy that takes into consideration the functionally and sectorally specific effects of local institutions and policies. It does this through an examination of the regional impact of Irish environmental protection regulation. In particular we focus on the effects of Cork County Council's regulation of the pharmaceutical sector. In the first section we discuss regional policy in theory and practice, and show how it is best defined in terms of an evolutionary system. This is followed by an analysis of the interaction between region-specific regulatory stringency and firms' capacity to respond to radical

[1] We would like to thank the participants of the Symposium entitled "A New Agenda for Irish Regional Development" held in UCC in September 2002 for their helpful comments that have improved this Chapter. Of course all remaining mistakes are our own. Some of the research in the Chapter was supported by an award from the Royal Irish Academy through the Social Science Research Committee Postgraduate Essay Competition. We would also like to thank the Academy for their valuable assistance.

changes in the regulatory environment. Our conclusion is that the Cork regional system's impact on local firms — in terms of their ability to respond to the new, more stringent national environmental regulations — was generally positive.

REGIONAL POLICY

Regional policy can be defined as the formulation by central government of funding, projects, regulations and other instruments, the objective of which is to impact unevenly on different parts of the country. Funding and projects, for example, are focussed on less advantaged places in order to reduce the gap between the level of development and prosperity in different regions of the country. The aim of these differentially impacting elements of policy is to offset or reduce the uneven development, which seems to be an inevitable consequence of the operation of markets.

In recent years rather than from the centre out — or from the top down — regional policy is being formulated more within the regions themselves. Both theoreticians and policy makers have supported this tendency. Among theoreticians Boschma and Lambooy (2002) argue that because development is uneven and location specific, regional policy must be "sensitive to local path dependencies, accounting for the particular technological, economic and institutional context". This approach, from an evolutionary economic perspective, suggests that policy for any particular region is best formulated and implemented by policymakers familiar with that region, ideally from within that region. Local governance through which links between firms and institutions can be enhanced to facilitate regional learning is supported by Morgan (1997) and Glasmeier (1999), among others. This is not to say that policy for a particular region can be formulated in isolation from national and even wider developments. "Cooke and Morgan (1998) have stressed the need to complement the region-specific strategy by a top-down approach (at the national or supranational level) that focuses on redistribution mechanisms" (Boschma and Lambooy, 2002). However, if top-down and bottom-up are the opposite ends of a continuum of types of regional policy, the recent literature has definitely shifted towards the bottom-up end.

Whether or not in response to these theoretical develop-ments,[2] governments have undertaken a similar shift; among other developments expressing this is the establishment of new, more local, governance structures. Regional Development Agencies have been set up in England and County and City Development Boards in Ireland. Academics of course continue to criticise regional policy and governance structures at various levels. One criticism is that these local agencies are too focus-sed on economic development. Related to this is the argument that all policies can have a regional impact. As Robinson (1999) puts it, "tackling economic, social and geographical division needs to be a fundamental aspect of all Government policy".

What we show in this chapter is that even environmental poli-cies and agencies can have regional aspects. The way that local authorities monitor and regulate companies' polluting activities can contribute to those companies' ability to respond to change. Policy (both industrial and environmental, in the case of the pharmaceutical industry in Cork) affected the evolution of the region and the consequence is greater competence within that region to adapt to changes in the extra-regional environment.

REGULATION AND FIRM COMPETENCE

The Irish approach to the environmental regulation of industrial activity changed radically in the 1990s with the establishment of a national Environmental Protection Agency (EPA) in 1992, and the introduction of Integrated Pollution Control (IPC) licensing in 1994. In its first year of implementing the new licensing the EPA was concerned solely with the licensing of the State's multina-tional bulk pharmaceutical manufacturers.[3] The IPC legislation included a schedule of licensable activities and a timetable for

---

[2] And, of course, it is at least possible that the direction of causality is the other way around.

[3] The identification of the pharmaceutical industry as the first priority for li-censing is a reflection of public concerns about the environmental impact of this industry.

phasing in the licensing of existing firms. The first sector to be licensed was firms employing more than 100 employees, or firms using a hazardous waste incinerator and falling within Class 5.6, "the manufacture of pesticides, pharmaceutical or veterinary products and their intermediates" (EPA, 1995, p. 41). Prior to the establishment of the EPA responsibility for the regulation of industrial activity was held by local authorities. It is generally acknowledged that Cork County Council had the most developed competence in regulating pharmaceutical manufacturers (McLean, 1997) and that the legislation was more strictly applied and enforced in Cork than in other local authorities (Moran, 1997). Seventeen pharmaceutical firms were licensed in this first phase (1994 and 1995), and this cohort (with the exception of one firm which was not included as the manufacturing process is markedly different) forms the basis for the research on which this chapter is based. The cohort is not large enough to provide a detailed exploration of the relative stringency of all nine local authorities with responsibility for these firms. However, by focussing on Cork County Council (responsible for seven of the firms) versus other local authorities (responsible for the remaining nine) we are able to ask whether there are differences in firm capability that are associated with the competence of the local authority and other institutional factors.

In the 1980s the European Community brought in directives to strengthen the prevention of pollution, introducing the requirement for BATNEEC (Best Available Technology Not Entailing Excessive Costs).[4] Emission limit values (ELVs) were set in water and air licence conditions and firms were obliged to demonstrate that pollution emissions fell within the limits. The ELVs set by regulators at that time were established with respect to available abatement technology, that is, end-of-pipe waste treatment equipment that ensured waste streams from the

---

[4] BATNEEC is a framework concept whereby regulators define the level of environmental control to be employed by firms based on what is technically achievable. Regulators must also take account of two sets of economic criteria: (a) the gains in environmental quality achieved weighed against the costs to industry (cost-benefit analysis) and (b) the affordability of these technologies in the sector (Sorrell, 2001).

production process were treated so as to comply with the permitted levels of emissions.

In issuing the first round of IPC licences to pharmaceutical companies in 1994/1995 the EPA issued revised BATNEEC standards for water emissions. The air emission levels were not tightened beyond the levels set in a 1987 Act, although the BATNEEC for air emissions was broadened to include pollution prevention technologies. In their application for an IPC licence firms were asked to identify whether or not they were in compliance with the BATNEEC standards, and where necessary to provide details of their plans to upgrade to these standards. For firms that had not achieved BATNEEC by the time of the IPC licence application the EPA made compliance a condition of the licence, specifying the pre- and post-compliance emission levels and the date for achieving BATNEEC. The IPC licensing process was therefore in effect a reassessment of the progress companies had made towards meeting their obligations under prior legislation. Firms that were previously licensed under the varying standards of interpretation and enforcement operating in different local authorities were, in the course of the IPC licensing process, measured against a uniform, national standard. This provides an insight into the impact of differing regulatory standards pursued by local authorities.

It can be seen from Table 8.1 that there is a clear and strong relationship between the stringency of the pre-IPC regulation and the state of the firm's pollution control technology at the time of IPC licensing. Data for this table, which are publicly accessible, were collated from the company IPC files held at the offices of the EPA (Hilliard, 2002). There is a statistically significant correlation[5] between the location of a firm and the achievement of BATNEEC in both air and water.

---

[5] The Kendall rank order correlation coefficient is 0.746, significant at the 99 per cent confidence level.

Table 8.1: Measures of Regulatory Stringency, Compliance and Dynamic Capability

Firms	Location	Water BAT-NEEC Compliance	Air BAT-NEEC Compliance	Strategic Development Capability
PHARMA C	Cork	✓	✓	4
PHARMA H	Cork	✓	✓	4
PHARMA K	Cork	✓	✓	3
PHARMA I	Cork	✓	✓	3
PHARMA F	Cork	✓	✓	2
PHARMA A	Cork	✓	✓	2
PHARMA B	Cork			0
PHARMA P	Non-Cork	✓	✓	4
PHARMA D	Non-Cork	✓		4
PHARMA E	Non-Cork		✓	2
PHARMA M	Non-Cork		✓	2
PHARMA L	Non-Cork			1
PHARMA N	Non-Cork			1
PHARMA G	Non-Cork		✓	0
PHARMA J	Non-Cork	✓		0
PHARMA L	Non-Cork			0

Source: Hilliard (2002, pp. 160 and 171).

- Seven of the 16 firms were compliant with both water and air BATNEEC at the time of IPC licensing.

- Of these seven firms, six were Cork-based firms; only one compliant firm had been regulated by a local authority other than Cork County Council.

- Nine firms had not complied with both water and air BATNEEC at the time of IPC licensing; only one of these firms had been regulated by Cork County Council.

This standardised BATNEEC evaluation suggests that a stringent regulatory regime will achieve a higher level of compliance with regulation: firms that were located in Cork were more likely to have technology in place to meet the emission limit values prescribed by the EPA in the new IPC licences.[6] However, central to the new licensing philosophy is continuous improvement and a shift of emphasis to pollution *prevention* rather than pollution *treatment.*

The main aim of IPC licensing is to stimulate the adoption of pollution prevention technology by firms. Pollution prevention technology, or cleaner technology, is defined as "approaches to manufacturing that minimise the generation of harmful waste and maximise the efficiency of energy use and material use" (Christie, 1995, p. 31). In cleaner technology, through changes to the manufacturing process, the generation of waste is avoided. The older, more traditional approach is end-of-pipe technology where waste streams emitted from manufacturing processes are treated to reduce or abate the toxicity of discharges to the environment so as to meet emission levels set by regulators.

Firms are required to meet standards for the emission of pollutants, as they were under the old licensing regime. But above that they are required to demonstrate a continuous effort to upgrade their environmental performance. Recognising that managerial processes are required to support cleaner technology uptake — "the common element is not technical but managerial – cleaner production is essentially a way of thinking about the energy and materials costs of a product and the impacts along the product's entire value chain" (Christie, 1995, p. 34) — licence conditions specify that firms put in place environmental management and information systems. Firms must also establish an environmental management plan (EMP) that sets goals and reports on progress. "The targets set are expected to be demanding of the licensee and require effort to achieve them" (EPA, 1998, p. 10).

---

[6] A participant at the Symposium suggested that this result could also be accounted for by environmentally weak, later entrants being strategic in their choice of location so as to avoid the strict regulation operating in Cork. There is no evidence to suggest that firms pursued this strategy. Of the seven firms that were established between 1980 and 1989, only two located outside the Cork region. Furthermore, estimating the correlation between age of plant and location, younger firms are more likely to be located in Cork (Hilliard, 2002).

One result of the new regulations for firms is that environmental management has become a strategic business issue. The IPC regulations are demanding, and reflect the regulator's intention to secure continuing reduction of environmental impact. Firms not only have to meet higher standards, they also have to change the type of technology they use, as well as implementing extensive environmental management and measurement systems. Firms that are not able to implement effective environmental management risk limiting their "flexibility of action" (Hoffman, 1997, p. 6), as the demands of the licence will act as a constraint on their activities. The EPA has strong powers to deal with non-compliance and can have a serious impact on a facility's operations. The most extreme sanction is that the EPA has the authority to close down a facility.[7] Non-compliant facilities also face other limits on their behaviour such as fines and court proceedings. Unannounced audits are used to investigate firms with persistent and unresolved problems. In these cases the EPA may oblige the firm to implement a particular solution or may compel the firm to cease a particular activity. Non-compliant companies are also named in the annual IPC report, and details of all problems are publicly available at the EPA. Community approval is also an important constraint for these plants. Plants that have not built trust with the community have found their flexibility of action constrained when it comes to obtaining official licences, such as planning permission and IPC licences. Firms that do not meet their IPC responsibilities are open to more than just EPA censure. The law is also open to the community: ". . . non-compliance with a licence, even in a minor respect, could destroy a defence to civil actions brought for damages" (Scannell, 1995, p. 1). Firms that have a strategic outlook recognise that they require an unofficial licence to operate from their neighbours.

Assessing the success of this new regulatory approach requires an assessment of firms' ability to comply with the requirements of the regulations and an understanding of the impact on firms of achieving compliance. The larger research

---

[7] This sanction has never been exercised by either a local authority or the EPA.

project from which this chapter is drawn (Hilliard, 2002) develops measures of the different elements of technical and managerial capability for responding to environmental regulations. These are suggested by both the literature on corporate environmental management and the theoretical literature on the evolutionary theory of the firm. In summary, this research establishes the role of organisational capabilities in determining a firm's ability to effect the necessary technical change and to manage the adaptation to a changed external environment.

The essence of the evolutionary theory of the firm is that the firm is a repository of knowledge, that this knowledge resides in the organisational capabilities of the firm and that these organisational capabilities then determine the firm's performance. Underlying capabilities are routines, routinised patterns of behaviour which are themselves both the products of and repositories of organisational learning and knowledge (Nelson and Winter, 1982). Organisational learning is an "intrinsically social and collective phenomenon" (Teece et al., 1994, p. 15), involving joint problem solving and co-ordinated 'search'. Although it may require the skills and knowledge of individuals, this still relies on "employment in particular organisational settings" (Teece et al., 1994, p. 15) for its expression. Organisational learning is also cumulative and path-dependent; what is learnt and practised is stored in routines — "the organisational memory of the firm" (Nelson and Winter, 1982, p. 99) — and expressed in the firm's capabilities. The ability to identify, develop and introduce new capabilities has been identified as an important capability in its own right, particularly important for managing the firm's response to change; "the term 'dynamic' refers to the capacity to renew competences so as to achieve congruence with the changing business environment" (Teece et al., 1997, p. 515).

The evolutionary theory of the firm has been used by a number of regional economists to develop theories of the "learning region" and "regional systems of innovation" (Morgan, 1997; Cooke et al, 1998; Maskell and Malmberg, 1999). The research discussed above on regional policy also supports these ideas. Focussing on the way evolutionary theory explains organisational learning, these writers argue that most firms learn from close interaction with suppliers, customers and rivals. Furthermore, processes of knowledge creation are strongly influenced by specific localised capabilities such as resources, institutions, social and cultural structures (Maskell and Malmberg, 1999).

We test this theoretical relationship between firms and their regional context in the discussion that follows. First, we provide a measure of dynamic pollution-prevention capability. Then we examine for correlation between dynamic capability and location.

Measuring capability is an attempt to measure complex, embedded, tacit and context-dependent patterns of knowledge and practice. This research uses data made available as part of the IPC regulations. The information available at the EPA is extensive; it includes the initial IPC licence application, monitoring results, reports of audit visits by the Agency, correspondence between the firms and the Agency and the firm's annual environmental reports. This rich data set allows the development of a set of measures of organisational capabilities that might be expected to have determined the firm's ability to meet the requirements of the new legislation. These measures capture (a) indicators of historical capability prior to licensing; (b) patterns of technical activity within the firm with respect to environmental technology; and (c) the development and operation of routines for management of environmental activity.

The research shows that not all firms will be able to respond to the new regulation as the regulators intend. Firms will be differentially successful in the take-up of cleaner technology solutions. They will also differ in the extent to which they have successfully introduced the managerial changes required by the regulators. The key finding is that firms with dynamic capability are more likely to have been successful in the development of managerial capabilities and are more likely to have been successful in the uptake of cleaner technologies. Dynamic capability in the context of response to IPC regulations is measured by examining the presence or absence of routines for information generation, problem identification and solution and strategic development. It corresponds to the search routines defined by Nelson and Winter (1982): routines for the identification and development of new routines. We have assessed each firm for evidence of environmental search routines. Table 8.2 outlines the criteria used to assign scores to each firm for dynamic organisational capability. The application of these measures to the 16 firms is presented above in Table 8.1.

Table 8.2: Criteria for Scoring Environmental Management Capability

Strategic Development *The systematic pursuit of continuous environmental improvement*	4	• Established routines for data collection and problem identification • Established programmes for generating pollution prevention projects • Established use of cross-functional continuous improvement teams
	3	• Systematic identification of pollution prevention projects • Recent introduction of continuous improvement teams • Integration of problem-solving capability into EMS
	2	• Recent/limited adoption of routinised data collection or problem-solving • Data collection without use in follow-up problem-solving
	1	• No systematic pursuit of pollution prevention • Evidence of environmental management problems due to incomplete information
	0	• Absence of pollution prevention projects • Explicit abatement only focus • Significant delays in IPC application process due to lack of information

Source: Hilliard (2002).

The question raised here, as a result of the broader research findings, is: Do regional factors influence firm-specific, strategic development capability? In other words, is there a regional competency that manifests itself in the development by firms of superior problem-solving capabilities, affording firms in that region an advantage in meeting the challenges of a new, demanding regulatory environment? The evidence is mixed. The statistical correlation between the stringency with which a plant was regulated historically and the possession of dynamic capability is significant only at the 90 per cent level of confidence.[8] Thus the correlation between location in Cork and BATNEEC compliance is stronger than that between location in Cork and dynamic capability but in both cases it would appear that location in Cork is important.

In relation to both these relationships, it should be pointed out that the small number of companies means that slight changes would significantly increase the statistical correlations. As we pointed out earlier, there are two companies that are different from others in their respective regions. Unlike other Cork companies, one, in our view, was neither BATNEEC compliant nor provided any evidence in its EPA file of having dynamic pollution-prevention capability. The other, unlike other non-Cork firms, was BATNEEC compliant and was unusual among non-Cork companies in being rated in our measure at the highest level of dynamic capability. If we remove these firms we obtain much stronger results, for both correlations.

CONCLUSION

We can conclude that apart from the few exceptions, there is evidence of a relationship between location in Cork and dynamic capability. What is the explanation, in this specific instance, for the relationship? Irish industrial policy — attracting multinational corporations to set up subsidiaries in Ireland — in relation to pharmaceutical and chemical companies was region specific, encouraging firms in this sector to locate in the Cork harbour area. Cork County Council was therefore responsible for a relatively large number of firms and this allowed them to

---

[8] The Kendall rank order correlation coefficient is 0.3024, significant at the 90 per cent confidence level.

build up greater resources and experience in enforcement. Expertise in environmental technology for the pharmaceutical industry was also developed in the local third-level institutes. Both University College Cork (UCC) and Cork Institute of Technology (CIT) have research centres in this area. The Clean Technology Centre (CTC) at CIT was founded in 1992 with funding from the pharmachem sector. The centre describes itself as "a strategic partnership between Irish industry and academia". It is recognised internationally as a centre of excellence in providing environmental consultancy and acting as "a national resource allowing all concerned with the environment to avail of a pool of expertise" (CTC, 2002).

Another effect of having a concentration of pharmaceutical firms was that the environmental performance of these firms became a high-profile issue for local citizens and the focus of NGO pressure. This external scrutiny provided increased impetus for rigorous enforcement by Cork County Council; it also provided pressure for industry self-regulation from responsible firms who did not want their reputation compromised by the actions of other firms. The former head of enforcement at Cork County Council, now Director for Licensing at the EPA, attributes it to "partly public pressure, partly NGO pressure, partly regulatory pressure and partly it was just the peer pressure" (McLean, 1997). A system evolved in which institutional interaction increased the levels of competency within firms, among their local regulators and the NGOs.

To return to the more theoretical explanation, as Cooke and Morgan (1998, p. 82) suggest, a region is a unique nexus of processes whose development is itself an evolutionary process.

> This process definition draws attention to the institutional and organisational means by which the region as a system of collective social order actually seeks to secure or switch its inherited regional path-dependencies by enhancing its capacity for learning (1998, p. 82).

The evolutionary theory of the firm provides a basis for understanding why some firms and not others were BATNEEC compliant and were able to develop beyond end-of-pipe pollution prevention to ongoing process improvement. The firms which did both had, in short, high levels of dynamic capability. And one of the reasons why these firms had high levels of dynamic capability was because they were in Cork, where interactions within the region enhanced the firms' capacity for learning.

References

Boschma, R. and Lambooy, J. (2002), "Evolutionary economic geography and regional policy: Escaping regional path dependency", Paper presented at the American Association of Geographers conference, Los Angeles, USA, March.

CTC, (2002), "Origin and Mission", Clean Technology Centre, Cork: http://www.ctc-cork.ie/aboutctc/frameabt.htm

Cooke, P., Uranga, M.G. and Etxebarria, G. (1998), "Regional systems of innovation: An evolutionary perspective". *Environment and Planning A*. Vol. 30, 1563-1584.

Cooke, P. and Morgan, K. (1998), *The Associational Economy: Firms, Regions and Innovation*, Oxford: OUP.

Christie, I. (1995), "The greening of industry: towards cleaner production in British manufacturing", *Policy Studies*, Vol. 16, No. 4, 29-48.

Environmental Protection Agency (EPA) (1995), *Report on IPC Licensing and Control 1995*, Ardcavan: EPA.

Environmental Protection Agency (EPA) (1998), *Report on IPC Licensing and Control 1997*, Ardcavan: EPA.

Glasmeier, A. (1999), "Territory-based regional development policy and planning in a learning economy", *European Urban and Regional Studies*, Vol. 6, No. 1, 74-84.

Hilliard, R.M. (2002), *Learning to change: The Role of Organisational Capabilities in Industry Response to Environmental Regulation,* Unpublished PhD Dissertation, Dublin: DCU Business School.

Hoffman, A.J. (1997), *From Heresy to Dogma: An Institutional History of Corporate Environmentalism*, San Francisco: New Lexington Press.

McLean, I. (1997), Director of IPC Licensing, EPA, Interview, June. In Hilliard, R.M. (2002), *Learning to change: The Role of Organisational Capabilities in Industry Response to Environmental Regulation,* Unpublished PhD Dissertation, Dublin: DCU Business School, p. 131.

Maskell, P. and Malmberg, A. (1999) "The competitiveness of firms and regions", *European Urban and Regional Studies*, Vol. 6, No. 1, pp. 10-25.

Moran, F. (1997), Director of the Federation of Irish Chemical and Pharmaceutical Manufacturers' Federation, Interview, May. In Hilliard, R.M. (2002), *Learning to change: The Role of Organisational Capabilities in Industry Response to Environmental Regulation,* Unpublished PhD Dissertation, Dublin: DCU Business School.

Morgan, K. (1997), "The learning region: Institutions, innovation and regional renewal", *Regional Studies,* Vol. 31, No. 5, 4491-503.

Nelson, R.R. and Winter, S.G. (1982), *An Evolutionary Theory of Economic Change*, Cambridge MA: Belknap Press.

Robinson, F (1999). "Region and Community: Balancing Regional Development and Community Regeneration". *New Economy,* Vol. 6, No. 3, 133-136.

Scannell, Y. (1995), "Some comments on IPC licences issued to date", Mimeo, Dublin: Centre for Environmental Law and Policy, TCD.

Sorrell, S. (2001), "The meaning of BATNEEC", *SPRU Working Paper No. 61,* Brighton: University of Sussex.

Teece, D.J., R. Rumelt, G. Dosi and S.G. Winter (1994). "Understanding Corporate Coherance: Theory and Evidence". *Journal of Economic Behaviour and Organization*, Vol. 23, 1-30.

Teece, D.J., G. Pisano and A. Schuen. (1997), "Dynamic capabilities and strategic management", *Strategic Management Journal*, Vol. 18, No. 7, 509-530.

PART 3

Ireland's Transport Infrastructure Deficit

Chapter 9

ACCESSIBILITY, TRANSPORTATION, INFRASTRUCTURE PLANNING AND IRISH REGIONAL POLICY: ISSUES AND DILEMMAS

Aisling Reynolds-Feighan

INTRODUCTION

Ireland experienced rapid and dramatic economic growth during the last decade. In the new millennium, Ireland faces opportunities and challenges to build on this growth, and must plan how economic opportunities and capacity will be distributed among the regions. The National Development Plan (NDP) sets out as a key regional policy objective, the reduction in disparities between and within the Border, Midlands and Western Region (BMW) and the Southern and Eastern Region, with sustainable development of both regions.

The purpose of the National Spatial Strategy (NSS) is to provide a detailed plan for the strategic development of the regions over a roughly 20-year planning horizon (NSS, 2002). The strategy will focus on the development of gateway centres as axes for sustainable growth in their regions (see O'Leary, Chapter 2 in this volume). A vital component at once driving and facilitating the realisation of this spatial plan is the transportation system.

This chapter focuses on the Irish transportation system and examines the issues and dilemmas facing the country in the next decade. There are significant deficiencies in the transportation networks at present and even with the very substantial investment planned under the NDP, economic agents face constraints and increased transportation costs in the procurement and distribution of goods and services, as well as in passenger movements.

In the next section of the chapter, the broad transport trends and needs are reviewed along with the forecasts prepared as background research for the NSS. In the third section, the European transport policy framework is outlined. The recent European Commission White Paper on Transport seeks to increase costs for road and air transport and effect an increase in the rail share of both passenger and freight traffic over the next 10 years. The suitability for Ireland of the policy stance adopted by the Commission is discussed in Section 4. The final section outlines key policy and institutional issues facing Ireland in the transport arena in the next 20 years.

TRANSPORTATION NEEDS AND RECENT TRENDS — A REVIEW

In this section, recent Irish transport trends are reviewed, with the aim of highlighting particular problems or challenges facing the national and regional economies in the next decade. Irish trends in infrastructure investment are briefly compared with other European countries.

Freight Trends

Accompanying the economic growth of the last 10 years has been a very dramatic increase in freight exports. Both Roll-on/Roll-off (Ro/Ro) or trailer traffic and Load on/Lift-Off (Lo/Lo) traffic have increased, with Ro/Ro rates of growth being greatest. The impact of these significant traffic changes has been felt at the main ports (particularly Dublin) and also along surface access routes to and from the ports.

Air freight traffic has increased substantially also, with a growing proportion of air freight being "air trucked" under air waybill to UK and European freight airports (most notably London-Heathrow, Amsterdam and Frankfurt). Dublin Airport accounts for 71 per cent of all airfreight, while Dublin Port

accounts for 75 per cent of all surface freight exports (Goodbody Economic Consultants, 2000a). Cross-Channel traffic
dominates the flow of goods to and from Ireland, but significantly, US traffic accounted for 17 per cent of exports and 16
per cent of imports in 2000 (Eurostat, 2002). Table 9.1 shows the
share of exports and imports by EU member states to partner
countries. Ireland along with Portugal and Luxembourg share
the lowest percentage of export trade *and* import trade with the
candidate countries.

Table 9.1a: External Trade by Member State and Partner, 2000

	Exports (€billion) to							
	Total Exports	*EU 15*		*EFTA*		*Candidate Countries*		*USA*	
B	204.0	151.8	74%	3.9	2%	6.7	3%	11.9	6%
DK	55.5	37.2	67%	4.0	7%	2.2	4%	3.3	6%
D	597.5	337.4	56%	30.6	5%	57.6	10%	61.8	10%
EL	11.9	5.2	44%	0.1	1%	2.5	21%	0.7	6%
E	124.8	87.7	70%	1.9	2%	5.5	4%	5.1	4%
F	351.8	216.2	61%	14.4	4%	14.9	4%	30.5	9%
IRL	83.8	53.0	63%	2.7	3%	1.7	2%	14.1	17%
I	260.4	144.4	55%	9.7	4%	20.4	8%	26.7	10%
L	9.1	7.6	84%	0.2	2%	0.3	3%	0.4	4%
NL	252.4	198.6	79%	5.9	2%	8.7	3%	11.1	4%
A	73.3	45.0	61%	5.2	7%	10.3	14%	3.7	5%
P	25.4	21.2	83%	0.6	2%	0.5	2%	1.5	6%
FIN	49.9	27.8	56%	2.2	4%	4.4	9%	3.8	8%
S	94.3	52.8	56%	8.4	9%	5.3	6%	8.9	9%
UK	308.5	175.8	57%	9.1	3%	10.3	3%	48.1	16%
EU15	2503.5	1551.4	62%	99.8	4%	151.3	6%	232.5	9%

Source: Eurostat (2002).

Table 9.1b: External Trade by Member State and Partner, 2000

	Imports (€billion) from								
	Total Imports	EU 15		EFTA		Candidate Countries		USA	
B	192.2	132.0	69%	3.7	2%	5.0	3%	14.4	7%
DK	49.3	33.7	68%	4.1	8%	2.2	4%	2.1	4%
D	538.3	295.3	55%	30.8	6%	50.8	9%	39.0	7%
EL	32.2	18.0	56%	0.5	2%	1.8	6%	1.2	4%
E	169.1	112.3	66%	2.8	2%	3.1	2%	7.4	4%
F	361.0	233.5	65%	17.5	5%	9.7	3%	26.7	7%
IRL	55.3	34.4	62%	1.4	3%	0.7	1%	8.9	16%
I	258.5	146.6	57%	9.3	4%	13.3	5%	13.5	5%
L	12.2	10.1	83%	0.3	2%	0.2	2%	0.4	3%
NL	236.3	120.8	51%	5.4	2%	6.2	3%	24.0	10%
A	78.4	53.9	69%	3.8	5%	9.4	12%	3.2	4%
P	43.3	32.5	75%	1.2	3%	0.8	2%	1.3	3%
FIN	37.3	23.1	62%	1.9	5%	2.0	5%	1.8	5%
S	78.9	50.7	64%	7.3	9%	3.5	4%	5.5	7%
UK	371.7	183.6	49%	18.1	5%	9.0	2%	49.5	13%
EU15	2513.9	1480.4	59%	108.3	4%	117.8	5%	199.0	8%

Source: Eurostat (2002).

Forecasts produced by Atkins McCarthy (2000) for the NSS suggest an 80 per cent increase in Ro/Ro traffic in the next decade, with Dublin Port experiencing the greatest share of the growth and volumes doubling in this timeframe. Airfreight in the same period is expected to increase by 150 per cent, but no forecasts are made of the air-trucking component. Boeing in their forecasts suggest that a substantial share of internal European air freight will be "air trucked" to major gateways by 2015 (Boeing, 2000), Irish air freight being trucked to UK and continental airports accounted for 21 per cent of total air freight in 1996. Irish air trucking has been proportionately higher than other European countries because of the relatively small size of aircraft operating in Irish markets (Reynolds-Feighan and Durkan, 1997).

The congested state of Dublin Port and Dublin Airport, along with the landside access constraints to these facilities have been highlighted in several recent studies (Atkins McCarthy, 2000; Goodbody Economic Consultants, 2000a, 2000b, 2000c). Congestion is affecting journey times and imposing delay costs on the movement of goods by road. Recent surveys by the Irish Business and Employers Confederation (IBEC) focus on the range of additional business costs affected by infrastructure congestion. Table 9.2 reports on the IBEC survey and highlights the labour market impacts of congestion. While the NDP will contribute towards reducing journey times and increasing short and medium term capacity of the National Roads network, Dublin Airport and Dublin Port, the forecast Ro/Ro traffic increases will exceed capacity by 2007 in Dublin Port, Lo/Lo traffic demand will exceed capacity by 2010, with Cork having capacity problems by 2004 (Atkins McCarthy, 2000). Spare capacity will remain available at Rosslare (Ro/Ro), Waterford (Lo/Lo) and Drogheda (Lo/Lo), and while there may be some scope in theory for redirecting traffic to these ports, in practice, carrier preferences will remain focused on Dublin. Airport capacity increases coming on stream in 2003-4 will be insufficient to cater for forecast demand in 2010. Nationally freight capacity through all ports will be exceeded by 2010.

Table 9.2: IBEC Survey Results of the Relative Impact of Congestion on Staffing (Percentage Reporting Adverse Impact)

	Dublin	Provinces
Staff Punctuality	94	68
Labour Costs	83	51
Recruitment	72	35
Staff Turnover	69	30
Absenteeism	62	29

Note: Based on responses from 580 companies, employing 67,000 persons.

Source: IBEC (2002).

Passenger Traffic Trends

Economic growth has substantially increased average incomes in a relatively short period of time. This affluence has increased demand for mobility and movement so that:

- Car passenger traffic has grown rapidly at ports

- Demand for air travel has dramatically increased, particularly on cross-channel and continental European routes

- Increased ownership of cars and participation in the labour force have given rise to congested road networks in urban areas particularly, with significant peak-period congestion extending over morning and afternoon/evening business hours

- Public transport provision at major ports and airports has been limited, so that road access congestion in the vicinity of these facilities has also grown steadily.

Ireland's geography, population density and dispersed settlement pattern have given rise to a heavy dependence on road and air transport. Table 9.3 shows the modal split for passenger traffic in the EU15 between 1970 and 1999. The growth in passenger car and the air transport shares, and the decline in rail transport's share have been widely reported. Figure 9.1 shows Ireland in 1999 as having the second lowest rail passenger traffic share. Figure 9.2 looks at the distribution of per capita Intra-European air traffic across the EU 15 in 1999. Ireland has the highest number of passengers per capita.

The reliance on air transport and low rail share for Ireland, Greece, Spain and Portugal is correlated with low population density and an urban system dominated by the largest city. For Ireland, maximum distances between the main population centres are below typical distances, where rail has a comparative cost advantage over road transport.

Table 9.3: Modal Split in EU15 (percentage of passenger-kilometres by mode of transport)

	Passenger Cars	Buses & Coaches	Tram & Metro	Railway	Air
1970	74.0	12.6	1.8	10.1	1.5
1980	76.2	11.6	1.4	8.4	2.5
1990	79.1	9.2	1.2	6.7	3.9
1995	79.5	8.7	1.1	6.1	4.6
1996	79.3	8.8	1.1	6.2	4.7
1997	79.3	8.6	1.1	6.1	4.9
1998	79.1	8.7	1.1	6.0	5.2
1999	79.0	8.4	1.1	6.1	5.4

Source: European Commission (2001).

Figure 9.1: Passenger Rail Share for EU15, 1999

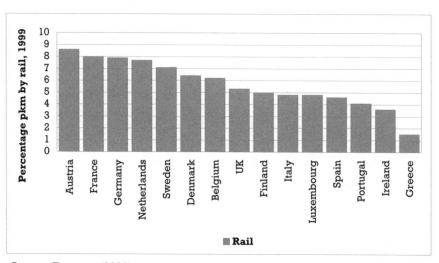

Source: Eurostat (2002).

Figure 9.2: Intra-European Enplanements and Total Air Passenger Numbers per capita, 1999

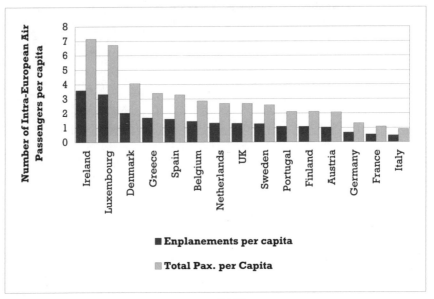

Source: Author's calculations; Eurostat (2002).

The recent report of the UK Commission for Integrated Transport included a comparison of delays caused by congestion across the EU in 1995. This comparison is summarised in Figure 9.3, which is reproduced from the Commissions report (2001). The figure shows that for Ireland, 13 per cent of links had delays of at least one hour, with 7 per cent having delays of three hours or more. From an Irish perspective, the UK data are also of considerable importance. The UK had the worst congestion in Europe, with almost a quarter of the most well used links experiencing delays lasting an hour or more. Several countries had no links at all with delays of an hour or more. These data are based on a Study from the European Centre for Infrastructure Studies (ECIS) undertaken in 1996. This study concluded that the UK's poor performance was a result of persistent underinvestment (ECIS, 1996).

Figure 9.3: Percentage of Links Congested

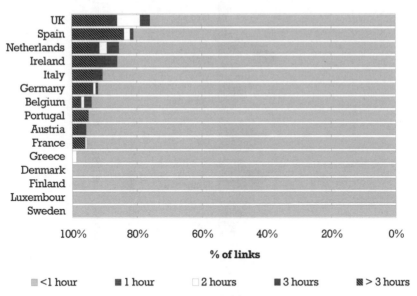

Source: Commission for Integrated Transport (2001).

Transport Infrastructure Investment

The NDP sets out a very substantial economic and social investment programme for the period 2000-2006. The investment strategy for the transport sector focuses on constructing and upgrading key road corridors between Dublin and Galway, Waterford, Cork, Limerick and the Border, construction of the Dublin Port Tunnel and a substantial public transport investment programme (most notably construction of the Luas light rail system in Dublin, upgrading of the Dublin suburban rail network and expansion and upgrading of the bus fleet). In the previous subsections, it was reported that even taking account of the NDP programme, significant capacity constraints will become binding over the next five years. The problems relate to both internal and external accessibility.

Figure 9.4: Per Capita Infrastructure Investment 1985-96

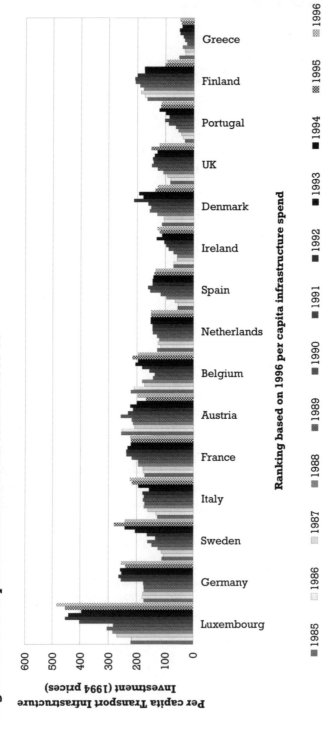

Source: Author's calculations based on Eurostat (2002).

Figures 9.4 and 9.5 give an overview of the pattern of transport infrastructure investment across the EU in the period 1985-1996. More recent data for all member states were not available. Figure 9.4 shows annual per capita transport infrastructure investments for each of the years 1985-96 for the EU15. Ireland is ranked 10th based on the 1996 per capita spend. Figure 9.5 shows the per capita infrastructure investment for the five years from 1990-95, and in this comparison, Ireland is ranked 13th of the EU15. While Ireland's per capita spend has increased in the late 1990s, the figure illustrates the sustained high spend on infrastructure in France, Italy, Germany, Austria, Sweden and Belgium. Finland and Denmark reduced significantly the per capita spend on transport infrastructure during the late 1990s.

Figure 9.5: Per Capita Infrastructure Investment, 1990–95 (ECUs)

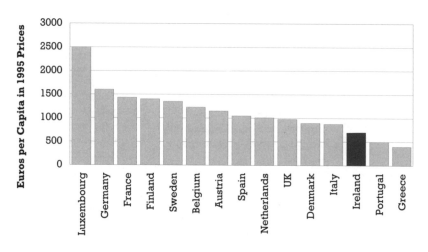

Source: Commission for Integrated Transport (2001).

EUROPEAN TRANSPORT POLICY

The White Paper on Transport, *European Transport Policy for 2010: Time to Decide*, was adopted by the EU Commission in September 2001. The new objectives set out for transport are summarised in the introduction by Loyola de Palacio as "restoring the balance between modes of transport and developing intermodality, combating congestion and putting safety and quality of services at the heart of our efforts while maintaining the right to mobility" (European Commission, 2001).

The main thrust of this white paper is to shift modal share in favour of rail by (a) Promoting the rail mode along with sea/inland waterways (b) Increasing the costs of road transport (c) Increasing the costs of air transport. A package of 60 policy measures is set out to achieve these objectives through regulations, harmonisation directives, user charges, taxes and investment strategies. Table 9.4 below briefly summarises some of the main measures for road, rail and air transport.

Table 9.4: EU White Paper Policy Initiatives Promoting Increase in the Rail Traffic Share

Mode	Measures	Impacts
Road freight	• Harmonising transport contract minima • Work-time regulations in road haulage sector • Road safety regulations • Imposition of road user charges	Raise the price of road transport and effect substitution in favour of rail
Rail	• Develop an internal European rail market with regulated competition • Rail safety regulations • Construction of dedicated rail freight network with community support • Develop rail network in "enlarged Europe"	Improve organisational and operational aspects in rail sector, increasing its attractiveness as substitute for surface and air transport
Air	• Creation of "single European sky" – reduce fragmentation of ATC • Harmonise and upgrade ATC equipment • Define new airport charges regulatory regime • Define environmental regulations/ rules • Imposition of fuel taxes (at least on intra-European services) • Promote intermodality with rail.	Increase operational costs in air transport and effect substitution of rail services for short haul air services Promote consolidation in European air transport industry Promote Spatial concentration of air traffic.

Source: European Commission (2001).

The White Paper proposes measures to encourage the emergence of freight integrators and to promote interoperability between rail and sea/waterway transport (such as the standardisation of containers and swap bodies). In dealing with the congestion problem, the Commission proposes the development of dedicated multimodal freight corridors along with expansion of the high-speed passenger network. The Commission also plans to propose a change in funding rules for the Trans-European Networks (TENs) increasing to 20 per cent the maximum contribution from the Community for cross-border projects crossing natural barriers and projects at the borders of candidate countries. In addition, it is proposed that in the next two years, a framework will be established for channeling revenues from charges on competing routes towards building new infrastructure, especially rail.

The European Court of Justice ruling in November 2002 found eight member states' "Open Skies" air service agreements with the US to be illegal (2002a and 2002b). EU Transport Ministers in June 2003 granted the European Commission the right to negotiate a common agreement with the US on behalf of all member states. The White Paper proposes a clear role for the Commission in negotiating a common external air transport policy and in facilitating increased spatial and industry concentration levels in the European airline industry.

ISSUES AND DILEMMAS FOR IRISH REGIONAL DEVELOPMENT AND THE FORMULATION OF A NATIONAL SPATIAL STRATEGY

A number of issues arise from the reviews of the previous two sections. Ireland has significant infrastructure capacity constraints that will impact on the performance of the national economy and the competitiveness and performance of the regions. The level of investment in transport infrastructure will need to be increased substantially if the productive capacities of the regional economies are to be expanded on a sustained basis.

The current levels of investment are insufficient to modernise and upgrade the national transport networks. Regional policy and regional/spatial planning operate to a much longer time span than national plans and must prioritise a programme of new construction and significant capacity expansion. Ireland is at present experiencing the mounting congestion and delay costs associated with short-run incremental increases in capacity. New funding mechanisms will have to be exploited to deliver substantial transport and productive capacity at reasonable cost for the regions and for the national economy over the next 20 years.

The European policy framework that has evolved for transport does not fit well with Irish transport needs and priorities. The Irish road network provides the basis for a flexible and extensive transportation network over which both public and private transport providers may operate. As an island and given the low population density, the dispersed settlement patterns and the dominance of Dublin in the urban hierarchy, rail transport has limited potential without very high subvention levels from regional or national government.

Research on long-run sustainable transportation options in low-density and non-contiguous regions and member states should be prioritised and inform a comprehensive European transport policy, suiting the differing needs of all major regions in the Union. At national level, government investment in transport research must be prioritised. Research supporting the key policy decisions that will take place in the next five years and shape the long term development of the island must be funded by national government with its own objectives, since these may differ from EU transport policy and research agendas.

The air transport policy agenda in Europe will have significant implications for Ireland, particularly given the relatively heavy reliance on this mode of transport. Research on US airline deregulation impacts has demonstrated the increased industry (or market) concentration among a small number of very large carriers *and* increased spatial concentration of traffic across a small subset of the airports network. In Europe, the development of high-speed rail networks and rail terminals at airports will free up slots at the large European airports, facilitating increased substitution of rail for short-haul air services.

The large European airports will service to an increasing extent, the long-haul external (i.e. extra-EU) routes. Changes in ownership requirements and the negotiation of common EU external aviation air service agreements (ASAs) will encourage both the increased concentration of traffic at the large airports, and increased industry concentration as consolidation among EU carriers takes place. Direct long-haul air links from Ireland to the US may be vulnerable under this scenario, although there is also the opportunity to increase the range of US destinations served directly from Ireland, rather than connecting through UK and other EU airports.

It is vital that a long-term Irish air transport policy be developed that meets regional development needs and national development priorities. The long-term provision of airport and port capacity needs to be addressed at regional and national levels. The regulatory and ownership structures for these facilities must be examined, so that bottlenecks and constraints do not restrict opportunities for enhanced accessibility or help make the case for reduced accessibility to and from Ireland. The impact of institutional structures on the transportation sector is an evolving research area in Europe and the US and this research effort has significant strategic implications for Ireland.

CONCLUSIONS

The NSS provides an important opportunity for Ireland to set out long-run strategic goals and plans for developing the regions and the national economy. Irish transport policy and the transportation system will play a significant role in facilitating and delivering economically and socially sustainable development over the next twenty years. Ireland's freight traffic is very heavily road-based and uses Dublin Port and Dublin Airport as key gateways to trading partners in the UK, continental Europe and the US.

Ireland along with the UK has a more substantial trade share with the US than other EU countries. Irish and US firms require direct airlift capacity between the two countries. The likely accession of some or all of the 13 candidate countries to the Union will move the European centre of gravity eastwards. The thrust of the EUs transport policy is to revitalise and expand the share of passenger and freight movements by rail, and to link, integrate and upgrade rail networks of the EU with those of the candidate countries. Ireland currently has very limited trade links with the candidate countries. While trade with continental EU countries has expanded significantly in the last decade, the UK trade and freight traffic shares dominate.

Forecasts of freight and passenger travel demand indicate that despite substantial investment, infrastructure capacity will be exceeded with 5 to 10 years. The NSS provides an important opportunity to set out a long-run plan for sustained large-scale investment in transport infrastructure and facilities.

Access to and from Ireland via the ports and airports will be constrained within 5 years. Ireland has the highest per capita air passengers in the EU along with the second lowest rail modal share. European transport policy over the next 10 years will seek to increase rail's traffic share and reduce the growth of air transport. The concentration of long-haul traffic at the large European airports and consolidation within the airline industry could have adverse effects on Ireland's regional and national development priorities. Irish aviation policy needs to be set out with the goal of facilitating the optimum development of air transport for the benefit of the regions.

Long-run planning of transport needs and policy goals will improve the efficiency of regional economies by reducing the substantial costs associated with a piecemeal and reactive approach. Transport policy in turn requires a broad research input to advise and inform optimum policy options.

References

Atkins McCarthy (2000), *Transport Corridors in Europe*, Study commissioned for the National Spatial Strategy, November.

Boeing (2000), *World Air Cargo Forecasts*, Boeing Commercial Airplane Company.

Commission for Integrated Transport (2001), *European Best Practice in Delivering Integrated Transport*, London, November.

European Centre for Infrastructure Studies (ECIS) (1996), *The State of European Infrastructure*, European Centre for Infrastructure Studies, Rotterdam.

European Commission (2001), *European Transport Policy for 2010: Time to Decide*, DG TREN, Brussels.

European Court of Justice (2002a), *Judgment 2002-11-05 (C-466/98) Commission v Royaume-Uni.* Available at http://curia.eu.int/jurisp/cgi-bin/form.pl?lang=en&Submit=Submit&docrequire=alldocs&numaff=C-466/98&datefs=&datefe=&nomusuel=&domaine=&mots=&resmax =100

European Court of Justice (2002b), *Opinion 2002-01-31 (C-466/98) Commission v Royaume-Uni.* Available at http://curia.eu.int/jurisp/cgi-bin/form.pl?lang=en&Submit=Submit&docrequire=alldocs&numaff=C-466/98&datefs=&datefe=&nomusuel=&domaine=&mots=&resmax =100

Eurostat (2002), *EU Energy and Transport in Figures*, Luxembourg: Eurostat Statistical Office.

Goodbody Economic Consultants (2000a), *Transport Demand*, Study commissioned for the National Spatial Strategy, November.

Goodbody Economic Consultants (2000b), *Sustainable Travel Demand*, Study commissioned for the National Spatial Strategy, November.

Irish Business and Employers Confederation (IBEC) (2002). Transport and Logistics Council Survey, Dublin, March 2002. Available at http://www.ibec.ie/ibec/press/presspublicationsdoclib3.nsf/7ddce1f 4694b8d9e802568d200532a90/3981081fd2be96fc80256bfa004adf16/$ FILE/National%20Traffic%20Congestion%20PR.pdf.

National Development Plan 2000-2006, (2000), Dublin: Stationery Office.

National Spatial Strategy for Ireland 2002-2020: People, Places and Potential (2002), Dublin: Stationery Office.

Reynolds-Feighan, A.J. & J. Durkan (1997). The *Impact of Air Transport on Ireland's Export Performance,* Institute of International Trade of Ireland, Dublin.

Spatial Planning Unit (2000). *National Spatial Strategy, Consultation document*, SPU, Department of the Environment and Local Government, Dublin.

Chapter 10

THE ROLE OF AIRPORT INFRASTRUCTURE IN REGIONAL DEVELOPMENT: THE CASE OF CORK AIRPORT

Ella Kavanagh, Eoin O'Leary and *Edward Shinnick*[1]

INTRODUCTION

Since it was founded in 1961, Cork Airport[2] has been a key infrastructural resource in the highly impressive growth of the South-West region of Ireland.[3] It has acted as a gateway for tourists entering the region, assisted tourists traveling abroad and has facilitated both business travel and exporting companies in the South-West. Since 1977 passenger numbers have grown by 7.6 per cent per annum to reach 1.9 million in 2002. In recent years this impressive growth has put pressure on airport facilities, requiring major infrastructural investment in the form of an extension to Cork Airport, which is on track for comple-

---

[1] This Chapter is based on a consultancy study on Cork Airport by the authors for Aer Rianta Cork (Kavanagh et al, 2001). The authors would like to thank Joe O'Connor, Director and John Smith, Marketing Manager of Aer Rianta, Cork Airport for assistance in data collection. The views expressed here are those of the authors alone.

[2] Cork Airport is the third largest airport in Ireland. It is managed by Aer Rianta, a semi-state company, which also manages both Dublin and Shannon Airports.

[3] This Regional Authority area comprises the counties of Cork and Kerry.

tion in 2005. At the same time, its external environment has changed significantly. The appointment of an airport regulator in 2001, responsible for regulating airport charges and the current discussions regarding ownership of the airport has introduced change and uncertainty. The key issue facing Cork Airport is how to satisfy its current and future infrastructural needs and continue to act as a catalyst for regional development in the South-West region, in the context of this changing environment.

The chapter continues by outlining how Cork Airport has been a crucial infrastructural facility in the growth of the South-West region. Section three uses a survey based input-output model to measure the impact of Cork Airport in the South-West region. This is followed in section four by an outline of the opportunities facing Cork Airport arising from airline deregulation. Section five deals with the case for new investment at Cork Airport and the crucial issue of financing such investment. The final section offers conclusions and recommendations on the appropriate future strategy for Cork Airport to continue its role in the development of the South–West region.

CORK AIRPORT IN A GROWTH REGION

Cork Airport is located in the South-West which is Ireland's second most prosperous region, after Dublin-Mid-East. Gross value added per capita in this region was 34 per cent greater than the EU average in 2000 (Central Statistics Office, 2003). Since 1960, the South-West has been one of the fastest growing regions in Ireland. During this period it has been transformed from an agriculturally based traditional economy to a high-technology export orientated regional economy of the "Celtic Tiger". Exports from the region are now fuelled by foreign owned electronics and pharmaceutical sectors located predominantly in the Cork area, and the indigenous food processing and tourist industries located throughout the region.

By international standards, Cork Airport is a small regional airport.[4] Passenger numbers have grown to reach 1.9 million in 2002. This compares to 15.1 million in Dublin Airport and 2.4 million in Shannon Airport. As Figure 10.1 shows, passenger growth has been particularly impressive in both Cork and Dublin since the early 1990s, averaging 10 per cent per annum since 1992. The performance of Shannon is considerably less impressive, with average growth over the same period of 3.5 per cent per annum. This is partly explained by the loosening of Shannon's transatlantic stopover agreement in the mid-1990s.

Figure 10.1: Passenger Growth in Aer Rianta Airports, 1977–2002 (1977 = 100)

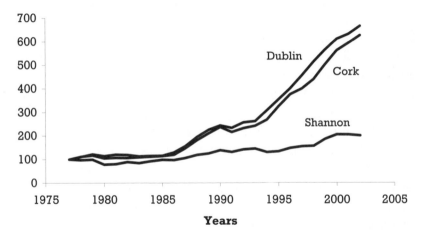

Source: Aer Rianta, Various Years.

The most important source of passengers using Cork Airport originate from the UK, which accounts for 57 per cent of traffic. The rest of Europe accounts for 24 per cent of traffic with the remainder being domestic traffic (19 per cent). By linking the South-West with the rest of Ireland, Europe and the rest of the world, Cork Airport has contributed to regional development in three ways. First, it has acted as a gateway for tourists entering

---

[4] This is based on the categorisation used by Airport Council International, which defines a small regional airport as having less than 5 million passengers (York Consulting, 1998).

the region. Tourist numbers to the region, which is Ireland's second most popular destination after Dublin, increased by 7.7 per cent per annum between 1995 and 2000, reaching 1.8 million. However, there was a significant drop of 18 per cent in the following year due to the "foot and mouth" outbreak in the country (Bord Failte, 2000 and 2002). A considerable number of new scheduled routes have opened in recent years to serve the main tourist markets of the UK and mainland Europe.[5] However, the other significant market, the US, is not served directly by Cork Airport due to restrictive bilateral agreements favouring Shannon Airport.

Second, Cork Airport has facilitated Irish tourists traveling abroad. For example, the number of passengers on sun charters increased by 23 per cent annually since 1997, resulting in over 50 sun flights each week. This growth reflects the "Celtic Tiger" boom in the Irish economy, with disposable incomes increasing by 8 per cent per annum during the late 1990s, high income elasticities for services and reduced family size (Duffy et al, 1999). Finally, the airport has provided the necessary infrastructure for exporting businesses located in the region. Business passengers have increased by 9 per cent annually since 1995. This reflects the strong growth of the South-West economy, where the export oriented foreign owned pharmaceutical and electronic sectors in the Cork area account for one third of regional output (Garhart et al., 1997). The expansion in availability of the key business routes to Dublin, London and mainland Europe has also facilitated this rise, although a direct service to the US would improve the situation.

As regards future growth, it is already clear that the Celtic Tiger growth rates of the late 1990s have not been sustained, with growth in the last two years averaging 4-5 per cent per annum. This slowdown, which was expected as the economy neared full employment and experienced high factor costs and infrastructural bottlenecks, was also influenced by sluggish

---

[5] These include services to Alicante, Barcelona, Belfast, Brussels, Cardiff, Milan, Malaga, Nantes, Nice, Prague, Rome and Swansea. Routes to Liverpool and London City will start later in September 2003. Clearly these may serve the business market also.

growth in the international economy. At a regional level, fore-casts conducted in 1999 indicate that output growth in the South-West would decline from the 8 per cent per annum be-tween 1995 and 2000 to 5 per cent over the following five years (O'Connor, 1999). In the context of the slowdown already un-derway, it is likely that these estimates are slightly optimistic. A more realistic scenario is growth in the region of 3-4 per cent per annum over the next few years.

Clearly this downturn will also affect future passenger num-bers at Cork Airport. As regards incoming tourists the expecta-tion is that growth will continue to slow. For business traffic, the overall slowdown in the regional economy is likely to have a direct impact on reduced passenger growth. However, the trend towards smaller families, relatively low unemployment and increases in the standard of living should continue to bol-ster the growth in Irish tourists travelling abroad. Overall, it is reasonable to expect that annual passenger growth to 2005 may decline to around 6-7 per cent per annum from the impressive 10 per cent achieved between 1992 and 2002. This forecast as-sumes that the expansion in airport capacity takes place in suf-ficient time to avoid airport congestion, which would otherwise undoubtedly slowdown passenger growth. Passenger numbers would be expected to exceed these forecasts over the next few years if the number of new routes continues to expand. For ex-ample, the recent launch of the Cork-based airline, Jetmagic, will boost passenger numbers.

THE REGIONAL IMPACT OF CORK AIRPORT

Cork Airport employed a full-time equivalent of 913 persons on-site in 1999. A total of 30 businesses were involved in activi-ties such as flight operation, freight handing, car hire, catering, retailing and public services. The regional impact of an airport not only includes on-site activity, but also income and employ-ment linked to the airport in terms of indirect and induced im-pacts. The former refers to activity linked to the airport through purchases by airport businesses in the region, the latter to the spending that occurs within the region out of the income accru-ing from the direct and indirect impacts.

These economic impacts were estimated for the year 1999 using an input-output model of the region that was originally developed by Garhart et al. (1997) and up-dated in a report by Kavanagh et al. (2001). Based on detailed surveys of on-site businesses, this report estimated that the indirect and induced employment multipliers were 1.22 and 1.27 respectively, giving an overall multiplier of 1.49 (Kavanagh et al., 2001).[6] Thus, an estimated 1,364 jobs were linked to Cork Airport in 1999. This compares to an estimated 702 jobs by Moloney et al. (1997) for 1995. The increase of 94 per cent in the regional impact of Cork Airport is due to employment increasing from 500 to 913 over these four years.

The overall employment multiplier of 1.49 for Cork Airport is similar to the estimate of 1.52, which was produced by Meyler (1995) in a study of the impact of Dublin Airport on the regional economy of North County Dublin. The estimate is on the lower end of the range of estimates from international studies. For example, in a survey of impact studies of thirty, mostly European airports, York Consulting (1998) report multipliers in the range 1.3 to 2.4. Similarly, Hart and McCann (2000) report larger multipliers for Stansted and other large UK airports. The relatively low value for Cork Airport is due both to the small size of the South-West, with a population of 556,000 in 1999, and to its extreme openness, with imports being 96 per cent of regional GVA (Garhart et al., 1997).

In addition to the impact of the airport itself, it may also be argued that an airport is linked to tourist spending in the region and to businesses located in the region owing to its presence as a key infrastructural facility. The peripherality of the South-West and the absence of other airports in the region reinforce the importance of these effects in this case. For example, Kavanagh et al. (2001) report from a survey of 800 non-resident passengers, that 40 per cent stated they would not have traveled to the region in the absence of an airport. This study also analysed the tourism impact by means of the expenditure patterns of those surveyed. It is estimated that a total of 2,826 jobs

---

[6] The report contains a detailed discussion of the data and methods used. Both multipliers referred to above are expressed relative to the direct impacts.

were linked directly to this expenditure. The indirect, induced and overall multipliers associated with this direct impact were 1.13, 1.28 and 1.41 respectively, giving a total of 3,973 jobs linked to Cork Airport in 2000 from the tourism impact (Kavanagh et al, 2001). This is very similar to the overall value of 1.40 produced by Tucker (1997) for the impact of Shannon Airport in the Mid-West region. Although this is a significant impact, it should be remembered that it refers to the regional impact of the travel and tourism industry, which includes the airport (York Consulting, 1998).

Finally, the airport could form part of the reason why inward investment is attracted to a region, why existing foreign or indigenous businesses are retained in a region or why businesses grow in a region. Most of the research on this issue, which has been referred to as the catalytic impact by York Consulting (1998), is qualitative, involving surveys of business attitudes on the role of the airport on location and competitiveness. No such work has been conducted on Cork Airport. However, it is clear that this effect is likely to be important in Ireland. For example, in a survey of thirty factors influencing competitive performance in large multinational firms based in Ireland in 1997, Hannigan (1998) reported that corporate managers ranked air and sea facilities sixth in order of importance.

The opening of a business park at Cork Airport in 1999 represents a tangible example of businesses linked to the airport in this way. By 2003, employment had reached 1,800, in businesses such as software consultancy, pharmaceutical research, financial and risk management services. Despite the downturn in economic activity, further expansion is already underway and expectations are that employment will expand to 3,000 by the end of 2005. A further tangible example of business links is EMC^2, which manufactures data storage systems and employs 1,100 persons in Ovens on the outskirts of Cork City. This business leases a hanger at Cork Airport where a private jet is based to transport international customers to and from the Cork plant. Therefore the airport is clearly linked to jobs at EMC^2. The company is unlikely to have located in Cork in the absence of an airport. However, other factors are clearly involved in the success of EMC^2.

Overall, Cork Airport has a significant impact in the region. Nearly 1,400 jobs were linked to airport activities in 1999. A further 4,000 jobs were linked to the airport as part of the travel and tourism industry. These impacts may be extrapolated to 2005, using the forecasted passenger growth, which based on the analysis in the previous section, are expected to slow to 6-7 per cent per annum to 2005. Such an extrapolation involves making assumptions about the employment density at the airport, which stood at 608 jobs per million passengers in 1999. Employment density may be expected to increase after the airport investment plans are completed, as the extended airport would result in an increase in the number of jobs at the airport. Assuming an increase to 850 jobs per million passenger, which is the indicative ratio for small regional airports used by Airport Council International (York Consulting, 1998), then Cork Airport would be linked to 2,800 jobs with a further 8,200 jobs linked to the travel and tourist industry in 2005. If this forecast is met, the already significant impact of Cork Airport in the regional economy of the South-West will be substantially larger in the next number of years.

OPPORTUNITIES FROM AIRLINE DEREGULATION

The de-regulation of the airline industry resulting in the liberalisation of air routes within Europe has created tremendous opportunities for Cork Airport. The greater competition and the resulting reduction in airfares has increased the demand for air travel and expanded the number of routes and capacity on existing routes. According to Reynolds-Feighan (1999), two of the most significant developments in Europe since liberalisation have been the development of low-cost carrier services and the increasing congestion at European airports. Both of these represent significant opportunities for Cork Airport.

In 2001, one low cost carrier, Ryanair, operated out of Cork Airport to London Stansted accounting for 47 per cent of all London Traffic. Cork Airport can continue to grow its market by encouraging low cost carriers, who rely on fast turnaround times in order to keep costs down. This is more difficult to achieve at congested airports. Congestion and shortages of runway space at the larger airports can result in growth opportunities for smaller airports like Cork, as airlines may switch to more direct flights and develop alternative (mini) hubs, if space is more readily available. Caves and Gosling (1999) highlight a trend towards the dispersion of routes in response to passengers' preference for direct routes and suggests, from UK experience, that international routes from small airports may be profitable with as few as 10,000 passengers per annum.

These growth opportunities for Cork Airport are highlighted in a survey of passengers and on-site businesses (Kavanagh et al., 2001).[7] Of passengers interviewed, 24 per cent requested more provincial UK routes, mostly to the north of England and to Scotland, while only 8 per cent requested more availability on the London route. A total of 38 per cent called for more routes to the main European capitals, with the main emphasis on routes to Germany (16 per cent), France (15 per cent), Brussels (14 per cent) and Spain (12 per cent). These routes would appeal especially to the low-cost carriers. Significantly 17 per cent requested direct access to east coast locations of the US, especially Boston or New York. The restrictive bilateral agreement favouring Shannon will cease when the EU takes over the responsibility of negotiating access with the US authorities, under a new "open skies" policy. It is significant that Aer Lingus has already expressed an interest in serving the US out of Cork when this new policy is introduced.

Cork Airport has responded to passenger needs in this changing environment by attracting a number of new airlines to Cork over the past two years. These include low-cost carriers such as flybe, Bmi baby and Aer Arann. In addition, Air Wales has established services to Cardiff and Swansea, Czech Airlines launched a new route to Prague, Aer Lingus launched a new route to Malaga and a new Cork-based airline, Jetmagic, has set up direct services to 13 destinations.

---

[7] Both surveys were conducted as part of the consultancy study by the authors for Aer Rianta Cork Airport. The passenger survey was distributed to 1498 people traveling out of Cork in the spring of 2000. The 30 businesses located in Cork Airport were surveyed in early summer 2000. For further details, see Kavanagh et al. (2001).

A further implication of deregulation and the subsequent increase in the number of alliances between national airlines is the development of hub airports. The opportunity for a regional airport like Cork is to try and compliment existing hubs by offering feeder services. This would mean expanding routes to Amsterdam, Dublin, London, Brussels and Paris, in addition to developing a new direct route to Frankfurt. The demand for such services is supported by the passenger survey (Kavanagh et al., 2001).

NEW INVESTMENT AT CORK AIRPORT

In order to realise its potential, new investment is required at Cork Airport to respond to existing needs and to assist further regional development. Doganis (1992) indicates that typically unit costs for airports fall sharply as traffic throughput increases, particularly up to 1.5 million passengers. It then levels off at around 3 million passengers. However, airport congestion is one factor that can cause unit costs to increase significantly. This implies that the optimal time for making capital investments is estimated to be approximately 1.5 to 2 million passengers. Clearly Cork Airport with 1.9 million passengers in 2002 is approaching the upper end of this threshold level and at current growth rates is expected to surpass 2 million passengers in 2003.

Kavanagh et al report the results of a survey of on-site businesses and passengers conducted in Cork Airport in 2000 (2001). This highlights the need for new capital investment and identifies specific gaps in the facilities the airport. On-site businesses recognised the need for more space in the terminal building, better customer facilities and more car parking. Inadequate cargo facilities were also noted along with the need for a longer runway to accommodate bigger aircraft. Passengers indicated that additional investment was needed in airport facilities including the need for a larger terminal building, air bridges to and from the aircraft and more shopping facilities. Cork Chamber of Commerce and a consortium of business interests in Cork have also argued for new investment in the airport to meet customer demands for enhanced facilities and ensure that Cork Airport is not at a competitive disadvantage.

Aer Rianta has also recognised the need for the new investment with their announcement in 2001 of a €140 million expansion of Cork Airport which will increase capacity to 3 million passengers when completed. Due to political uncertainty in relation to the ownership structure of the airport, there have been delays in the building programme. However, it now appears to be on track for completion in 2005.

An important issue facing Cork Airport is how to generate sustained future revenue growth in order to fund current and future investment needs. The two main sources of revenue for an airport are aeronautical and non-aeronautical revenue. Aeronautical charges are paid by the airlines and include landing fees, passenger charges and aircraft parking fees. Non-aeronautical revenue arises from passengers and business at the airport. It is generated by commercial activities in the terminal and on airport land. These include, rents from airlines, car hire, taxies, catering, banks, income from concession shops, fuel concession and car parking fees. Revenue from these commercial activities can be used to support aeronautical charges.

It should be noted that the removal of duty free sales for intra-EU passengers in June 1999 had serious consequences for the generation of revenue at the Aer Rianta managed airports of Cork, Dublin and Shannon. Aer Rianta was one of the most exposed European airport groups to the loss of EU duty free with some 85 per cent of passenger traffic being intra-EU compared to 59 per cent for BAA (Warburg Dillon Read, 1999). The loss of revenue has been particularly significant for Cork Airport with almost 96 per cent of passengers, who were previously EU and eligible for duty free, now becoming "domestic" (i.e. within the EU) compared to 88 per cent in Dublin and 63 per cent in Shannon (Aer Rianta, 1999). Before the removal of duty free, revenues obtained through duty free sales were used to reduce aeronautical charges and fund airline discount schemes to encourage them set up new routes. The removal of duty free has cut off this important source of investment funding at Cork Airport.

More recently the appointment of an Airport Regulator has implications for the relative roles of aeronautical and non-aeronautical sources of revenue to finance investment in Cork Airport. These will now be dealt with in turn.

Aeronautical Revenue

With the Aviation Regulation Act 2001, an Airport Regulator has the responsibility for "regulating airport charges and aviation terminal charges" for the three airports managed by Aer Rianta in, Cork, Dublin and Shannon. Aer Rianta's airport charges have traditionally been below average compared to other European airports. For example, the European Airport Landing Charges Index developed by Symonds Travers Morgan's placed Aer Rianta's charges as the third lowest out of 20 airport pricing schemes in 1998 (British Airport's Authority, 1998/9). These lower charges have contributed to the recent growth of Cork Airport by providing airlines with lower start-up costs, thereby enabling airlines to establish routes and not incur heavy losses while doing so.

In setting aeronautical charges, the statutory objective of the Commission for Aviation Regulation is "to facilitate the development and operation of cost effective airports which meet the requirements of users" (Aviation Regulation Act, 2001). In fulfilling its statutory objective the regulator is obliged to have due regard to ten specified statutory factors, one of which concerns taking into consideration "the contribution of the airport to the region in which it is located" (Aviation Regulation Act, 2001). This was reinforced in 2001 by a direction from the Minister for Public Enterprise, Ms. Mary O'Rourke, to the Commission "to make every reasonable effort to ensure that its final determination reflects the important emphasis which the Government has placed on balanced regional development".[8] It is clear from the Act that the statutory objective of cost effective airports takes precedence over the statutory factors. This is

---

[8] This quote is taken from a letter sent to the Commission for Aviation Regulation by the Minister in August 2001. In particular in this letter the Commission was referred to (i) the National Development Plan 2000-2006 and one of its four objectives of "fostering of balanced regional development" and (ii) the National Spatial Strategy and one of its key principles of "the creation of the right conditions for the balanced regional development to take place by developing the potential of areas in the regions to create and sustain economic strength in a structured way" (Commission for Aviation Regulation, 2001b, pp. 29/30).

consistent with the view of the airport as a commercially oriented profitable concern.

The key role of the Regulator is therefore to set aeronautical charges to meet the capital investment needs of users and ensure that there is a reasonable rate of return on the capital employed, thus enabling sustainable and profitable development of the airport. The first decision of the Regulator in 2002 took the form of a "price cap", which set an upper limit on aeronautical fees. The fee is then adjusted upwards on an annual basis to take account of the annual inflation rate, minus the so-called "X" factor, which reflects efficiency improvements.[9] In setting aeronautical charges, all non-aeronautical revenue is considered by the Regulator. This "single-till" approach effectively allows for cross-subsidisation of aeronautical by non-aeronautical activities, within the Aer Rianta group (Commission for Aviation Regulation, 2001a and 2001b).

For the first year, of the five-year period beginning 2001/02, the Regulator set a maximum yield from airport charges for Aer Rianta's three Irish airports taken together of €6.34 per passenger.[10] A separate maximum yield from airport charges of €5.38 per passenger was set for Dublin Airport (Commission for Aviation Regulation, 2002). If the upper bound (€6.34) is binding, then this suggests that the maximum yield from airport charges is on average higher for Cork and Shannon at €7.30 per passenger.

Two aspects were considered by the Regulator in setting fees. First, Dublin Airport requires resources to alleviate congestion and bottlenecks. Second, both Cork and Shannon Airports need continued investment to promote sustainable development in their regions and to act as counterbalances to Dublin (Commission for Aviation Regulation, 2001b). The objective seems to be to provide Dublin with sufficient revenue

---

[9] For the three Aer Rianta airports taken together, the annual "X" factor has been set at 5 per cent whereas for Dublin it has been set at 7 per cent. This suggests continued lower maximum charges for Dublin airport relative to Cork and Shannon airports.

[10] These maximum charges are due for review in August 2003.

for further investment and ensure that its development will not be restricted by subsidising Cork and Shannon Airports.[11]

To achieve balanced regional development, regions like the South-West and Mid-West need to grow faster than Dublin/Mid-East, which is Ireland's most prosperous region. However if the higher maximum aeronautical charges are adopted by Aer Rianta, the attraction of Cork and Shannon Airports may be reduced relative to Dublin. This, in turn, could negatively affect the expansion of Cork and Shannon and therefore their important role in regional development. The assumption here is that airlines are responsive to relative price changes. There is ample evidence of this, especially in relation to low-cost carriers. For example, Ryanair frequently claim that higher charges in Ireland are inhibiting its expansion in the country.[12] This claim has been supported by Ryanair's recent decision to transfer the majority of its Shannon-Frankfurt flights to Kerry instead of Shannon because of lower charges in Kerry. It has earlier been argued that these low-cost airlines represent an important opportunity for growth for Cork Airport.

These demand-side effects are therefore important in setting charges. However the Commission seems to have concentrated more on supply-side effects in its determination. That is, higher fees can fund infrastructure investment under the doubtful assumption that these higher fees will not deter airlines using the airport. In turn, the balanced regional development issue is addressed by the claim that inefficient infrastructure will undermine regional gateways (Commission for Aviation Regulation, 2001b), the implication being that cost effective airports is the over-riding objective. Thus, while the Regulator's current maximum fee schedule is consistent with its statutory objective of the Commission, it may be inconsistent with the goal of balanced regional development. If the government is serious about achieving balanced regional development then

---

[11] The degree to which any such subsidies have occurred in the past is not clear since Aer Rianta does not publish separate account for their three airports.

[12] *Irish Times*, 1 March 2001.

the statutory objective of the Commission for Aviation Regulation should be amended to fully reflect this.

Non-Aeronautical Revenue

The implicit assumption of the Regulator's approach is that airports are a commercial entity. This suggests that in the current regulatory environment, Cork Airport will need to focus on generating non-aeronautical sources of revenue from commercial activities at the airport if it is to have competitive charges. According to Doganis (1992), for all airports, even the smaller ones, which are more heavily dependent on aeronautical charges, generating more commercial revenues is attractive because it presents fewer difficulties than trying to increase aeronautical revenue. More and more airports are turning to such commercial activities to generate revenue for investment. For example, British Airports Authority's (BAA) revenue is dominated by non-aeronautical activities as over 70 per cent of its revenue is from "non airport and other traffic charges" (British Airport's Authority, 1998/9).

At present, non-aeronautical revenue accounts for approximately 50 per cent of Cork Airport's total revenue. This level is low by international standards. Increasing this source of revenue will provide future investment funding for Cork Airport and enable it to charge lower aeronautical fees, thereby attracting further growth. Such a move involves developing a commercial strategy to enable Cork Airport to maximise revenue from this source, which, in turn, will enable it to continue to grow, thus enhancing regional growth. In this way it can also contribute to balanced regional development.

CONCLUSIONS AND RECOMMENDATIONS

Since it was founded in 1961, Cork Airport has been a key infrastructural resource in the highly impressive growth of the South-West of Ireland. It has contributed to its growth in three ways: by acting as a gateway for tourists entering the region, by facilitating Irish tourists travelling abroad and by providing the necessary infrastructure for exporting businesses located in the region.

A survey-based input-output model of the South-West region was used to determine the impact of Cork Airport. Based on surveys of on-site businesses, it was estimated that nearly 1,400 jobs were linked to Cork Airport in 1999. When account is taken of expenditure by tourists using the airport, a further 4,000 jobs were found to be linked to the tourism industry which includes Cork Airport (Kavanagh et al., 2001). Moreover, a considerable number of additional jobs are related to the airport in terms of its importance as a key infrastructural facility for businesses in the region.

Cork Airport requires new investment to respond to existing needs and to assist further regional development. Since 1992, the growth in passenger numbers has averaged 10 per cent per annum, which has put pressure on airport facilities. The need for investment is borne out by a survey of on-site businesses and passengers (Kavanagh et al., 2001), which identified specific gaps in the facilities at the airport. Moreover, Cork Airport requires further investment to enable it to continue to benefit from the opportunities resulting from the liberalisation of air routes. This need for new routes was also supported by the passenger survey (Kavanagh et al., 2001) and has seen the airport respond by attracting several new airlines and new routes from existing airlines.

Aeronautical fees for the three Aer Rianta airports in Ireland are set by an Airport Regulator. The Regulator has set lower maximum aeronautical fees for Dublin than either Cork or Shannon. It is argued that if higher relative fees are adopted at Cork Airport, then future airport growth may be inhibited thus negatively affecting regional growth in the South-West. In setting maximum fees the Regulator's statutory objective of facilitating the development of cost effective airports was achieved while the statutory factor of considering the role of the airport in the region was deemed to be met by providing efficient infrastructure. If the Government is serious about achieving balanced regional development then this must be made explicit in the Regulator's statutory objective, given the crucial importance of airport infrastructure to regional development.

The first key issue facing Cork Airport is how to generate sustained revenue growth to fund investment needs and enable it to continue to contribute to regional development. According to Reynolds-Feighan, (see Chapter 9 in this volume), new funding mechanisms will have to be developed to improve transport infrastructure in Ireland.[13] The first recommendation of this chapter is that a commercial strategy is put in place in Cork Airport. The possibility of higher maximum fees being adopted at Cork Airport highlights the need for the development of such a strategy to expand revenue from commercial activities based at the airport. The development of a new terminal building can facilitate this expansion by providing space for more retailing activities. Other European airports, such as Amsterdam and Frankfurt, have already undertaken such a strategy and this has pushed the contribution of non-aeronautical revenue to total revenue at these airports to well over 50 per cent. While Cork Airport is not a hub airport like Amsterdam and Frankfurt, it too has potential to increase the amount of commercial activity in the terminal building from its current low levels. This increased non-aeronautical revenue could then be used to maintain lower aeronautical charges, which in turn would stimulate airport growth. In this way Cork would continue to act as a catalyst for regional development.

The second key issue concerns the ownership of Cork Airport. Currently Aer Rianta manages the three airports of Dublin, Cork and Shannon. Current government policy, recently announced by the Minister for Transport, Mr Seamus Brennan, favours breaking up Aer Rianta and establishing separate management boards for Cork and Shannon. Given this policy, the second recommendation of this chapter is that in setting up an independent management board at Cork Airport, the objective should be to include regional stakeholders so that the airport may continue to play a key role as a catalyst for regional development in the South-West. This would provide the airport

---

[13] The decision to allow an independent operator to build a terminal for low cost airlines at Dublin airport represents an alternative way in which airports can expand their existing capacity and introduces an element of direct competition within an airport for the first time.

with greater freedom to develop a commercial strategy and pursue independent promotional and pricing strategies.

References

Aer Rianta, *Annual Reports*, Dublin: Aer Rianta, Various Years.

Aviation Regulation Act (2001), Dublin: Government Stationary Office.

British Airport Authority (1998/9), BAA Annual Report and Accounts, www.baa.co.uk.

Bord Fáilte (2000), *Tourism Facts 1995-1999 — South-West Region*, Dublin: Bord Failte.

Bord Fáilte (2002), *South West Facts 2001*, Dublin: Bord Fáilte.

Caves, R. and Gosling, G. (1999), *Strategic Airport Planning*, Amsterdam: Elsevier Press.

Central Statistics Office (2003), *County Incomes and Regional GDP*, Dublin: Central Statistics Office.

Commission for Aviation Regulation (2002). *Published Decisions on Airport Charges:Press Release.* 11th Feb, www.aviationreg.ie.

Commission for Aviation Regulation (2001a), *Determination in respect of Maximum Levels of Airport Charges that may be levied by an Airport Authority in respect of Dublin, Shannon and Cork Airports*, Commission Paper CP7/2001, www.aviationreg.ie.

Commission for Aviation Regulation (2001b), *Report on the Determination of Maximum Levels of Airport Charges – Part 1,* Commission Paper CP8/2001, www.aviationreg.ie.

Doganis, R. (1992), *The Airport Business*, London: Routledge.

Duffy, D., Fitzgerald, J., Kearney, I. and Smyth, D. (1999), *Medium Term Review, 1999-2005*, Dublin: ESRI.

Garhart, R., Moloney, R., O'Leary, E. and Donnellan, T. (1997), *An Input-Output Model of the South-West: A Preliminary Report,* Department of Economics: UCC Working Paper Series, 97-7.

Hannigan, K. (1998), "The Business Climate for Multi-national Corporations in Ireland", *Irish Banking Review*, Autumn, 2-14.

Hart, D. and McCann, P. (2000), "The Continuing Growth of London Stansted Airport: Regional Economic Impacts and Potential", *Regional Studies* Vol. 34, No. 9, 875-893.

Kavanagh, E., O'Leary, E. and Shinnick, E. (2001), *The Role of Cork Airport in Regional Development: Strategic Opportunities,* Report Commissioned by Aer Rianta, Cork Airport.

Meyler, A. (1995), *The Social and Economic Impact of Dublin Airport,* Report Commissioned for Aer Rianta Dublin Airport.

Moloney, R., Garhart, R., O'Leary, E., Donnellan, T. and Twomey, M. (1997), *The Economic Value of Cork Airport: An Input-Output Study of the Impact of Cork Airport On Its Catchment Area,* Report Commissioned by Aer Rianta, Cork Airport.

O'Connor, J.F. (1999), *The Irish Regions: Review and Medium-Term Forecasts 1996-2005*, Dublin: ESRI Working Paper No. 120.

Reynolds-Feighan, A. (1999), "Deregulation of the European Air Transport Sector: Impact and some Implications for Ireland", *Irish Banking Review*, Winter, 12-25.

Tucker A. (1997). *Shannon Airport Impact Study*, Report for Mid-West Regional Authority.

Warburg Dillon Read (1999), *Review of Strategic Options for the Future of Aer Rianta,* Report Commissioned by the Minister of Public Enterprise and the Minister for Finance.

York Consulting (1998), *The Economic Impact of Airports,* Report Commissioned by Airport Council International.

Chapter 11

CENSUS COMMUTING DATA AND TRAVEL TO WORK AREAS: AN EXPLORATORY ANALYSIS

Michael J. Keane[1]

INTRODUCTION

The geographic association of economic and social conditions is a classic regional science question (Web Book of Regional Science, 1999). Research and policy interest in topics like core-hinterland interdependencies and intraregional linkages was strong 30 years ago with the promotion of the growth centre approach to regional development (Hansen, 1972; Berry, 1973; Buchanan 1969). However, this approach gained only temporary popularity because the "trickle-down" of economic activity from the growth centres to their hinterlands turned out to be, in many cases, no more than a trickle (Barkley et al., 1996). Hansen (1990, p. 32) has summarised aspects of the debate and discussion around these concepts and noted that "critics with a rural-agricultural orientation tended to regard the growth centre approach as unduly urban in nature, while more urban oriented critics complain that the designated centres are too numerous, too small, and too unpromising". Hansen also argues

[1] The work presented in this chapter is part of a research project on Urban–Rural Interaction supported under the PRTLI Cycle 2 research programme of the HEA.

that economically beneficial "spread" or "trickle down" effects between centres and their hinterlands were scarcely in evidence. This debate reached a critical stage in Ireland in 1969 with the publication of what became known as the Buchanan Report (Buchanan, 1969). This consultancy document, commissioned by the national government as an aid to the development of a regional policy, proposed a regional planning strategy that was based on a hierarchy of growth centres. These recommendations were endorsed by many bodies and by the government's own advisory agency of that time, the National Industrial Economic Council (Keane, 1984). The government, however, decided against taking the actions recommended by the consultants and, by default, continued with a policy aimed at "an overall regional strategy" which basically sought to promote a fairly even spread of economic activity around the country (Industrial Development Authority, 1972).

The tendency in recent years for economic activity and opportunities to agglomerate in larger urban centres has forced planners and policy-makers to re-examine the growth centre question. The recently published National Spatial Strategy (NSS, 2002) has proposed a spatial development framework based on selected "gateway" and "hub" urban centres serving functional economic areas (FEAs). These gateways and hubs are described as "strategic centres with the potential to be drivers of development at national level and within their own regions" (NSS, 2002, p. 38). However, this concentration of activity and effort can be detrimental to the development prospects of small towns and rural areas unless we can be sure that significant spread/linkage effects from the designated strategic centres exist. Another implication of economic activity wanting to agglomerate spatially is to lengthen travel-to-work journeys due to an increasing separation of places of residence from places of work. Longer commuting distances have become an economic and social concern in Ireland in recent years as employment opportunities become more separated from places where people live. Data from the Census of Population and the Quarterly National Household Survey show how the numbers travelling to work over 15 miles has increased from 8.2 per cent of the total in 1991 to 10.9 per cent in 1996 and 12.4 per cent in 2000.

Garreau (1991) describes what he calls a long-standing law of commuting: "scholars have demonstrated for thousand of years, no matter what the transportation technology, the maximum desirable commute has been 45 minutes". Taking this "law" literally, it suggests that economic areas be limited to specific ranges of distance. The distance that defines an FEA is linked to two things: the degree to which growth disseminates geographically and to Garreau's law of commuting. Wheeler (2001) provides us with some evidence on the range for economic areas in the USA — Metropolitan Statistical Areas (MSAs) with an average radius of 22 to 27 miles and Component Economic Areas (CEAs) extending up to 50 miles from a central node. The lack of suitable data sets makes this kind of geostatistical analysis difficult to conduct in Ireland. All that we seem to be able to do is offer very ad hoc notions about functional regions and possible spread effects. A good example can be found in the ESRI's National Investment Priorities for the Period 2000-2006 (Fitzgerald, et al., 1999), which contains a map of catchment areas for the main cities, defined in terms of 30 and 60 minute driving times. The most recent suggestions about economic areas are the functional areas outlined in the National Spatial Strategy (NSS). Some of these areas, such as the Western FEA, are presumably identified in terms of some notion of a commuting catchment area but there is no information as to the methodologies used in delineating these areas. They are constructed to represent sets of places that "have characteristics in common and share inter-relationships in the way they function economically and socially (NSS, 2002, p. 75) but how these relationships are established in the NSS is not at all clear or easily understood.

Acknowledging from the outset that the particular proposals are only indicative outlines, there is a striking lack of congruence between the ESRI's 60 minute travel-to-work areas and the FEA in the NSS. Taking Galway city as the focus we can add two additional "definitions" to the discussion. The first is associated with the planning study entitled, the Galway Transportation and Planning Study (GTPS) prepared by Buchanan and Partners (1999). The consultants took a very pragmatic approach to the notion of Galway and its economic hinterland by simply defining the Study Area as extending 30km from Galway city. The second is the local authority's settlement strategy map, which shows service hubs and strategic sector boundaries. There is an acknowledgement in the *Draft Development Plan* (Galway County Council, 2002) that Galway city is the key economic driver in the whole region whose influence extends beyond the county boundary. However, the so-called strategic sector boundaries are nothing other than the local electoral areas adjusted for the GTPS study area boundaries. Thus, we have a number of operational concepts, none of which are grounded in any kind of concrete analysis of how spatial policy areas might look like and how they should be constructed (van der Lann et al., 2001). There is a challenge to find appropriate concepts for describing urban and rural areas, which can be used to mobilise attention and perform policy work.

It is difficult to capture the concept of the FEA precisely. By its very nature an FEA will not have definite boundaries. The dynamics of different activity spaces and relational networks are constantly jostling together so areas will be different and they can change. As Healey (1996) notes, all places are becoming increasingly fragmented into an amalgam of what she describes as "bits and pieces" and "niches and nodes". The evidence that is most typically considered in defining functional economic areas is commuting patterns (Johnson, 1995). The modern concept of functional urban regions (as applied in Europe) is based on a commuting hinterland of 15 per cent of the working population (Hall and Hay, 1980; Cheshire et al., 1995). Bennett (1997) warns that, while this 15 per cent is important, it does omit the working activity space of the 85 per cent of the population who work elsewhere. Furthermore, the working population is only usually about 40 per cent of the total population. Clearly, most people may have totally different activity space based on leisure, social, public and private service demand and supply which do not fit with the commuting workplace, which can be a great distance away. These "more local" activity spaces may also be more relevant for administration since they relate more closely to the larger users of public services that are locally supplied. The identification of spatial policy areas that will reflect functional spatial ties and describe urban and rural areas can help planners working on territorial development plans (Galway Co. Council, 2002).

The focus of this chapter is on the shape and strength of functional areas. Its purpose is to examine travel-to-work data using Exploratory Data Analysis (EDA) methods in order to see if it is possible to gain some insights into the scale of functional regions. The data used were especially extracted from the 1991 Census of Population. Galway city and the eastern part of the county are the focus in this empirical exploration of spatial structure and pattern. The data used was made available by the Central Statistics Office as a special run from the 1996 Census of Population.

An Analysis of Census Commuting Data

While the Census commuting data may provide a general perspective on contemporary patterns of commuting (Horner, 1999), it is difficult to work with this data set in a rigorous manner. It suffers from a number of serious limitations. The first is that the data set does not contain information about origin/destination or direction of travel, it only tells us about the commuting behaviour of individuals in terms of distances travelled and transport modes used. The second difficulty with the data set is the way in which it is organised. This can be seen in Table 11.1, which displays the data for one District Electoral Division (DED), the Ahascragh DED. The two obvious problems evident from this table are the way in which the responses are classified into groupings with uneven-sized intervals and the sometimes high number of not-stated responses to the census question on distances travelled to work.

***Table 11.1: Travel to Work Data for Ahascragh District
Electoral Division: 1991***

Unadjusted Data (miles)										
Total	0	1	2	3	4	5-9	10-14	15-24	25-29	50+	Not Stated
195	81	4	1	4	4	66	5	3	8	0	19

Grouped Data (miles)						
Total	1-4	5-9	10-14	15-24	25-29	50+
105	14	73	6	3	9	0

Source: 1991 Census of Population: Special run of DED travel-to-work data

Note: DED No 153 in Figure 11.1.

This chapter looks at the data with EDA methods. In order to make the data workable two adjustments were made: the not-stated responses were distributed proportionately across the different distance categories, the zero category was ignored and the remaining data was grouped. These are shown in the bottom part of Table 11.1. From the adjusted data approximate values of medians and interquartile points etc. could be calculated using grouped data methods (Shao, 1972). The full number of DEDs are shown in Figure 11.1. There are 178 DEDs included in the EDA exercise.

EDA is concerned with resistant identification of data properties (Tukey, 1977; Hoaglin et al., 2000) and is a useful approach in trying to identify spatial arrangements or evidence of functional structure using the Census commuting data. The main EDA tool used is the box-plot. A display of parallel box-plots of batches of data for eight different randomly selected DEDs is shown in Figure 11.2.

Figure 11.1: DEDs of East County Galway

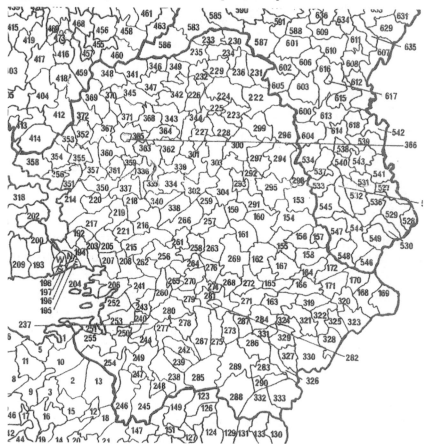

Source: O'Cinneide and Cawley (1983), 205 = DED code number

Figure 11.2: Box-plots for Census Commuting Data

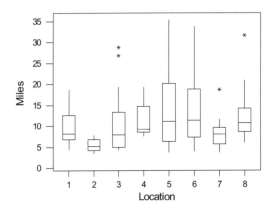

To construct a box-plot for a batch of data we draw a box with ends at the lower and upper quartiles and a crossbar at the median. Next, we draw a line from each end of the box to the most remote point that is not an outlier. The resulting figure schematically represents the body of data minus the outliers. Each outlier is represented by an ($*$) symbol situated beyond the outlier cutoffs. An observation y_i is classified as an outlier if:

$$y > F_u + 1.5(F_u - F_l): \text{ or } y_i < F_l - (F_u - F_l)$$

where F_l is the lower quartile, F_U the upper quartile and $(F_u - F_l)$ the interquartile range. The tails of the box-plot are determined primarily by the most extreme data values that are within the outlier cutoffs. The box-plot shows at a glance the location (median), spread (interquartile range), skewness, tail length and outlying data points and it allows us to see similarities and differences among the batches with respect to each of these features. For example, the median distance is smallest for DED 2 as is the amount of variability. This suggests that there is a fairly coherent pattern in travel-to-work distances with most distances close to the median. For DED 4 the median is much closer to the lower quartile indicating that the batch is positively skewed. The suggestion for this batch of data is that while there is a high degree of variability (especially above the median, note the upper tail) in distances travelled, there is a strong concentration of distances just below the median. DEDs 5 and 6 display the greatest amount of variation with only a slight positive skewness. Generally, the value of the box-plot is its ability to convey visually some important information about the shape of the different batches of data.

A comparative feature in Figure 11.2 is the tendency for spread to increase as the median (level) value does, or vice versa. This relationship is quantified by fitting a regression line using the ordinary least squares estimator and computing the R^2 goodness-of-fit measure (see Figure 11.3). The *t*-ratio for the slope coefficient is 3.18. There is evidence of a statistically significant relationship. The reverse of this relationship is also worthy of attention. The spread gives an indication of the range of distances that people travel from a particular DED. A priori, the expectation is that as this range increases so will the typical (median) distance travelled. Keane (2001) has developed a simple model of search and commuting distances which suggests that this relationship will be non-linear. This result is supported in the data (see Table 11.2).

Figure 11.3: Plot of Spread against Median

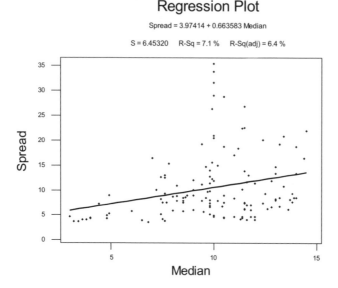

Regression Plot

Spread = 3.97414 + 0.663583 Median

S = 6.45320   R-Sq = 7.1 %   R-Sq(adj) = 6.4 %

Table 11.2: The Relationship between Spread and Median Distance

Regression equation 1.	Median = 8.75 + 0.107 Spread	$R^2 = 6.4$
Regression equation 2.	Median = 6.21 + 1.67 Logspread	$R^2 = 11.4$

A further exploratory question is to what extent do neighbouring DEDs exhibit similar commuting behaviour? Figure 11.4 shows plots of m_j, the median value for DED_j, against $(Wm)_j$, where $(Wm)_j$ is the median of the DEDs that share a common boundary with area j. This is labelled as Lag in Figure 11.4. The plots in Figure 11.4 do indicate a strong relationship between neighbouring values. The relationship is quantified by fitting a regression line using the ordinary least squares estimator and computing the R^2 goodness of fit measure. The t-ratio for the slope co-efficient is 8.22.

Figure 11.4: Plot of Median against the Average of Neighbouring Values

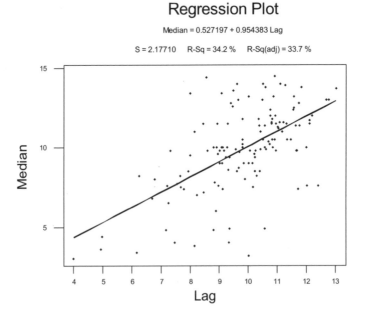

Regression Plot

Median = 0.527197 + 0.954383 Lag

S = 2.17710   R-Sq = 34.2 %   R-Sq(adj) = 33.7 %

It is interesting to see if commuting behaviour follows a trend with respect to distance from Galway City. Figure 11.5 shows a series of box-plots for groups of DEDs that are grouped in terms of "lagged" distance from the city. The DEDs that share a common boundary with the city are at distance band 1, all the DEDs that have common boundaries with the DEDs at distance band 1 are at distance band 2 and so on. There are 11 such distance bands shown in Figure 11.5. The plots in Figure 11.5 do not allow for direction. In addition, the number of DEDs falling into each band are quite variable. The pattern shown in Figure 11.5 can be interpreted with the help of some additional information in relation to the location of key settlements. For example, the distance bands 5 and 6 contain towns such as Tuam, Loughrea and Gort and the modulating effect that they have on travel distances can be seen. The town of Athenry is the outlier in band 4 in Figure 11.5. Beyond band 6 there is much variability in distances and no discernible trend in levels.

Figure 11.5: Box-plots with Distance from Galway City

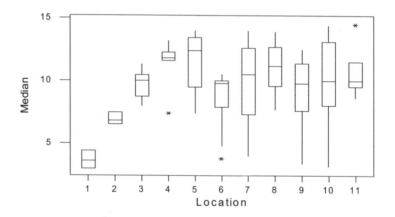

DEFINING COMMUTING PATTERNS USING NOTCHED BOXPLOTS

In Figure 11.2 there are differences between medians. Using the concept of a notched box-plot it is possible to determine confidence intervals among the medians. McGill et al., (1978) contains a full description of the statistical background to determining these notch widths. The notches surrounding the medians provide a measure of the statistical significance of differences between the values. Specifically, if the notches about two medians do not overlap then the medians are significantly different at an 95 per cent confidence level. With this tool it is possible to look for DEDs or sets of contiguous DEDs whose median values are significantly different from those adjacent to them. Significant differences are used to confirm patterns or significant disjunctures in the commuting data. The picture of the region that we get is shown in Figure 11.6. The contour like lines in Figure 11.6 connect DED(s) that are contiguous and whose medians are statistically the same. The median values for DED(s) on one side of each contour are statistically different from the values on the other side. Thus, these contour lines indicate significant breaks in travel distances and in the orientation of commuters.

The key features highlighted in Figure 11.6 include:

- A robust commuting area extending from Galway City. Figure 11.6 shows a nicely behaved series of statistical breaks in the values of the median distance travelled as distance from Galway increases, which help to define this region. The strength of this travel-to-work area is moderated by Tuam in the north/north-east and, to a lesser extent, by Gort in the south. It is difficult to say with the data how far exactly the city travel-to-work area extends beyond the last statistical break between 11.8 and 16.1 miles, but it does appear to be quite open-ended. A statistical break can be detected just north of the N-63 which suggests a possible outer limit. Loughrea town has only a modest impact on the median values and there are no further statistical breaks that indicate how far into south-east Galway the Galway travel-to work area extends other than to the outer boundaries of the Ballinasloe, and, to a lesser extend, the much smaller Portumna travel-to-work zones.

- A well-defined commuting field around Ballinasloe with considerable open-endedness in the north-west and western side sides of this sub-region.

- A small commuting travel-to-work area can be defined around Tuam. In addition, the town exerts a moderating impact on median distances throughout the north and parts of the north-east of the county.

Figure 11.6: Travel to Work Areas

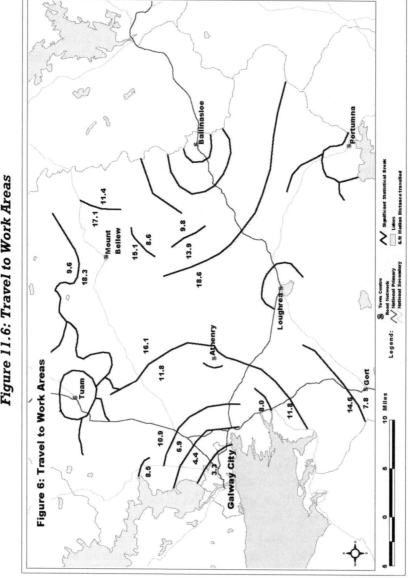

Figure 6: Travel to Work Areas

Despite misgivings about the Census data these features are reasonable and, from a policy perspective, offer a potentially interesting picture of the urban and regional dynamics. The EDA methods used have proven to be a useful tool in detecting and defining some significant geographical patterns in commuting behaviour which, in turn, helps to inform the definition of FEAs. The patterns are not precise and tidy, they are fragmented and there is a high degree of open-endedness in the kind of regions they help define. This result is not surprising as it would be impossible to expect a set of nicely behaved regions with closed boundaries. What is, perhaps, most useful about the whole exercise are the (relative) benchmarks that are identified in Figure 11.6. These benchmarks can be used, for example, to look at the issue of changes in the scale of economic processes in the county over time. Is it to be expected, for example, that in the 2002 Census data there will be statistical evidence of an expanding Galway City region, a contracting Tuam and Ballinasloe region? This information about scale can be significant for the design of strategic interventions for different parts of the county.

CONCLUSIONS

The geographic scope for growth in aggregate economic activity and employment appears to be restricted to urban agglomerations. From a planning and policy perspective it does make sense that we recognise these trends and begin to think, as is suggested in the NSS, in terms of FEAs. The challenge then is to provide the information about what may constitute a functional area. It is difficult, if not impossible, to capture this concept precisely. By its very nature an FEA will not have definite boundaries. The dynamics and values of different activity spaces and relational networks are constantly jostling together so areas will be different, they can change, and there is no constant definition. Again, as Healey (1996) notes, all places are becoming increasingly fragmented into an amalgam of what she describes as "bits and pieces" and "niches and nodes". The challenge for researchers is to try and make some sense out of these fragmented patterns and to develop a policy focus on critical linkages, nodes and dynamics as understood in specific local contexts (Healey, 2002). This chapter has looked at the potential value of EDA methods in addressing these technical challenges.

Commuting data from the Census of Population is difficult to analyse. The data is made available on a DED basis and, as such, any DED variable will represent the average behaviour or condition existing within a local area. Also, the distribution of DEDs is very irregular (see Figure 11.1) and this makes for further difficulties in formally exploring distributional characteristics and other arrangement properties in the data. The EDA methods employed here appear to be quite successful in identifying some relatively robust functional configurations/disjunctures in the data. The findings provide benchmark information about what might constitute the limits of functional economic areas, which is useful for discussion and planning. The regional schemes cited in the introductory discussion are fairly gross characterisations but they are symptomatic of the way in which policy discussion and thinking is dominated by the economic performance of the large cities and by an unclear view as to what exactly the relationships between these large cities and their more rural hinterlands might look like. The opportunities and roles for the smaller settlements are largely ignored or they are poorly articulated in policy proposals. This position is well illustrated in the key recommendations found in the Galway Transportation and Planning Study (GTPS). This study, as mentioned earlier, took a pretty pragmatic approach to the notion of an FEA by using an arbitrary zone of 30 kms from Galway to define the planning region. The main thrust of the recommended planning strategy in the GTPS is the adoption of the Galway City-Oranmore corridor as the location for public infrastructure investment and new development. A case is also made for allocating a significant portion of growth to Tuam which, in the view of the consultants "can be distinguished from the other scheduled towns as a location which can not only absorb more development but which would greatly benefit from it." (Buchanan 1999, pp.4-13/4-14). To quote further from the GPTS:

> Even if the consultants are right in suggesting that economic priorities favour the location of growth in Galway

City east of the River Corrib, it does not follow that the development strategy should be based on this: there may be legitimate social factors which indicate that growth should be encouraged to locate elsewhere. The obvious candidates are the scheduled towns where it is argued that new employment opportunities are essential to reactivate communities suffering from depopulation and a lack of resources, and whose further development would take pressure off Galway City and the roads leading to it.

This is a persuasive scenario, and one put forward in the most recent report by the Western Development Commission. However, in the consultant's view, it has to be queried on a number of grounds. First, even if thought desirable, it is, in the consultants opinion, unlikely to prove feasible. Little of the assumed employment would be willing to by-pass Galway in favour of an apparently peripheral location even if substantial additional (and expensive) incentives were to be offered. This view is supported by local experience, if the scheduled towns have not expanded during the past decade of unprecedented growth and subsidy, they are unlikely to do so now when both have probably peaked.

Second, it is possible to question the need for the diversion of new employment to outlying areas; to suggest, in fact, that such a strategy is perhaps rather unthinkingly aimed at returning those communities to their previous role rather than adapting them to a new role as dormitory towns to Galway city. Such a role could well be the natural successor in a situation in which economic forces are giving yet another change of direction to the physical structure of the Study Area. There are innumerable examples elsewhere of prosperous satellite communities enjoying more peaceful existence in superior environmental conditions while exporting a high proportion of their citizens to work in less congested surroundings in the parent city. In a local context, it could be said that the inhabitants of the scheduled towns are lucky to have Galway City to turn to for employment and higher-level services: without it, they would be in a much less favour-able position.

Third, it is possibly wrong to imagine that the importance of new employment is the only way to revitalise satellite communities. Both experience elsewhere and the surveys conducted locally by the consultants show that most people do not live close to where they work and that, increasingly, sub-regions such as the Study Area are becoming single social and labour markets in which a large number of travel networks, including home-to-work trips, overlap each other as people move in all directions to access a variety of services. What we see is not a number of inward looking self-contained activity centres, but a highly mobile population looking for good access to whatever the area as a whole can offer. It is therefore legitimate to envisage a situation in which new employment is allowed to settle down as it wishes, while housing and its associated uses are encouraged to locate in the scheduled towns, as is currently happening in places like Tuam where developers and buyers are seeking to benefit from the lower land costs, and where the simple accumulation of people can generate more services. The emphasis can then switch to providing a good transportation system to ensure ready access between the various centres of activity (Buchanan, 1999, 4-13/4-14).

It is difficult to disagree with the economic logic used by the consultants. What they are suggesting is that the scale and intensity of the economic processes are such that the fates of the city and the adjacent communities have become more and more dependent. The analysis of travel-to-work patterns in Figure 11.6 goes some way towards defining the spatial shape and extent of this dependence. The key driving forces behind this contemporary spatial patterning are the priorities of national infrastructural investment programmes and the decisions of major companies and investors as to where to invest in private development projects. The recommended spatial strategy in the GTPS is to basically support and facilitate these decisions. The consequences, if this recommendation is adopted, will be to extend and further intensify the travel-to-work area of the city beyond the already extensive limits, as outlined in Figure 11.6. This will put pressure on roads and on transport systems and relegate the "so-called" scheduled towns to mainly service and residential roles. For something significantly different to happen in these towns any spatial strategy and the policies it adopts will need to have very persuasive power to influence key actors and very strong regulatory powers to offset the centripetal forces that are clearly dominant in the county.

The 2002 Census of Population commuting data will be published soon and with this data it will be possible to look at the more recent evolution of travel-to-work areas in the county. Commuting is a key linkage in the process whereby the economic growth that provides jobs in the urban centres can be transmitted into other parts of the territory. The EDA techniques applied to the commuting data can provide interesting insights on these types of processes. There is also an opportunity to extend the analysis to look at these processes at work in the context of the other gateways and hubs identified in the National Spatial Strategy.

References

Barkley, D.L., M.S. Henry and S. Bao. (1996), "Identifying 'Spread' versus 'Backwash' Effects in Regional Economic Areas: A Density Function Approach", *Land Economics*, Vol. 72, No. 3, 336-57.

Bennett, R.J. (1997), "Administrative Systems and Economic Spaces", *Regional Studies*, Vol. 31, No. 3, 323-336.

Berry, B.J.L. (1973), *Growth Centers in the American System*, Vol. 1, Cambridge, MA: Ballinger.

Buchanan, C. (1969), *Regional Studies in Ireland*, Dublin: Stationery Office.

Buchanan, C. and Partners (1999), *Galway Transportation and Planning Study*, London: Buchanan.

Cheshire, P., A. Furtado, S. Magrrini (1995), "Analysis of European Cities and Regions: Problems of Quantitative Comparisons", *Discussion Paper No. 108, Department of Economics,* University of Reading.

FitzGerald, J. et al. (1999), *National Investment Priorities for the Period 2000-2006*, Dublin: Economic and Social Research Institute.

Fitzpatrick Associates (1999), *Border, Midlands and Western Region Development Strategy 2000-2006*, Dublin: Fitzpatrick Associates.

Galway County Council (2002), *Draft County Development Plan*, Galway: Galway County Council.

Garreau, J. (1991), *Edge City: Life on the New Frontier*, New York: Doubleday.

Hall, P. and D. Hay (1980), *Growth Centres in the European Urban System*, London: Heinemann.

Hansen, N. (1990), "Growth Center Theory Revisited" In D. Otto and S.C. Deller eds. *Alternative Perspectives on Development Prospects for Rural Areas.* Proceedings of an organised symposium, annual meetings of the American Agricultural Economics Association, pp. 31-45.

Hansen, N. (1972), *Growth Centers in Regional Economic Development*, New York: Free Press.

Healey, P. (2002), "Urban-Rural Relationships, Spatial Strategies and Territorial Development", *Built Environment*, Vol. 28, No. 4, 331-339.

Healey, P. (1996), "The Communicative Turn in Planning Theory and Its Implications for Spatial Strategy Formation", *Environment and Planning B*, Vol. 23, 217-234.

Hoaglin, D.C., F. Mosteller and J.W. Tukey (2000), *Understanding Robust and Exploratory Data Analysis.* New York: Wiley.

Horner, A. (1999), "The Tiger Stirring: Aspects of commuting in the Republic of Ireland 1981-1996. *Irish Geography*", Vol. 32, No. 2, 99-111.

Industrial Development Authority (1972), *Regional Industrial Plans 1973-1977*, Dublin: IDA.

Johnson, K.P. (1995), "Redefinition of the BEA Economic Areas", *Survey of Current Business*, April, Washington: Department of Commerce.

Keane, M.J. (2001), "A model of commuting distances: Some preliminary insights for a model of spatial search", In *Transport Planning, Logistics, and Spatial Mismatch* ed. D. Pitfield, European Research in Regional Science, Vol. 11. London: Pion, pp. 169-177.

Keane, M.J. (1984), "Accessibility and Urban Growth Rates; Evidence for the Irish Urban System", *The Economic and Social Review*, Vol. 15, No. 2, 125-139.

McGill, R., J.W. Tukey and W.A. Larsen (1978), "Variations of Box Plots", *The American Statistician*, Vol. 32, No. 1, 12-16.

National Spatial Strategy for Ireland 2002-2020: People, Places and Potential (2002), Dublin: Stationery Office.

O'Cinneide, M. and M. Cawley (1983), *Development of Agriculture in the West of Ireland 1970-1980*, Dublin: Acot.

Shoa, S.P. (1972), *Statistics for Business and Economics*, Columbus Ohio: Merrill.

Tukey, J.W. (1977), *Exploratory Data Analysis*, Reading MA: Addison-Wesley.

Van Der Lann, L., and R. Schalke (2001), "Reality versus Policy: The Delineation and Testing of Local Labour Market and Spatial Policy Areas", *European Planning Studies*, Vol. 9, No. 2, 201-221.

Wheeler, C.H. (2001), "A Note on the Spatial Correlation Structure of County-Level Growth in the US", *Journal of Regional Science*, Vol. 41, No. 3, 433-449.

Web Book of Regional Science 1999. http://www.rri.wvu.edu/Web-Book.

INDEX